D0404566

BLUE/ORANGE

BY JOE PENHALL

★

★

DRAMATISTS
PLAY SERVICE
INC.

2

BLUE/ORANGE was first performed at the Cottesloe Theatre, Royal National Theatre in London, England, on April 7, 2000. It subsequently transferred to the Dutchess Theatre in London, England, on April 30, 2001.

BLUE/ORANGE received its New York premiere at the Atlantic Theater Company (Neil Pepe, Artistic Director; Beth Emelson, Producing Director) in New York City on November 20, 2002. It was directed by Neil Pepe; the set design was by Robert Brill; the lighting design was by Brian MacDevitt; the sound design was by Scott Myers; the costume design was by Laura Bauer; and the production stage manager was Darcy Stephens. The cast was as follows:

CHRISTOPHER .... Harold Perrineau, Jr.
BRUCE .... Glenn Fitzgerald
ROBERT .... eljko Ivanek

CHARACTERS

CHRISTOPHER

BRUCE

ROBERT

PLACE

The action takes place over twenty-four hours in a
modern psychiatric hospital in London.

TIME

The present.

BLUE/ORANGE

ACT ONE

A consultation room. A transparent cooler. A round table with a large glass bowl containing oranges. Bruce and Christopher stand facing each other.

CHRISTOPHER. Mister Bruce —
BRUCE. Christopher —
CHRISTOPHER. Mister Bruce —
BRUCE. How are you doing?
CHRISTOPHER. Brucey Brucey Brucey. How are you doing?
BRUCE. A pleasure as always.
CHRISTOPHER. A pleasure. Yeah a pleasure. The pleasure's all mine, man.
BRUCE. Take a seat.
CHRISTOPHER. The pleasure today is mine. D'you know what I mean?
BRUCE. Plant your arse.
CHRISTOPHER. It's mine! It's my day. Innit. My big day. What can I say…?
BRUCE. Yes well yes — sit down now.
CHRISTOPHER. Gimme some skin.
BRUCE. Why not. *(Bruce shakes Christopher's hand. Christopher makes it an elaborate one. They punch fists.)*
CHRISTOPHER. I'm a free man. D'you know what I mean?
BRUCE. Well … a-ha ha … OK.
CHRISTOPHER. I'm a happy man. Bursting with joy.

BRUCE. Chris?

CHRISTOPHER. Oh — hey — oh … OK. I'll be good. You're right. I should sit. *(Christopher sits with exaggerated calm.)*

BRUCE. Relax.

CHRISTOPHER. I should relax and calm myself.

BRUCE. Take a few breaths. Would you like some water?

CHRISTOPHER. *(Fidgeting.)* Uh?

BRUCE. Would you like a cup of water?

CHRISTOPHER. Coke.

BRUCE. No you don't have —

CHRISTOPHER. Ice cold Coke. The Real Thing.

BRUCE. No you know you can't have Coke —

CHRISTOPHER. Yeah I can because —

BRUCE. What did I tell you about Coke?

CHRISTOPHER. I'm going home tomorrow.

BRUCE. What's wrong with drinking Coke?

CHRISTOPHER. But I'm going home.

BRUCE. Chris? Come on you know this, it's important. What's wrong with Coke? *(Pause.)*

CHRISTOPHER. It rots your teeth.

BRUCE. No — well yes — and…? What else does it do to you?

CHRISTOPHER. Makes my head explode.

BRUCE. Well — no — no — what does it do to you really?

CHRISTOPHER. Makes my head explode — oh man — I know — I get you.

BRUCE. It's not good for you is it?

CHRISTOPHER. No. It's bad.

BRUCE. What's the first thing we learnt when you came in here?

CHRISTOPHER. No coffee no Coke.

BRUCE. No coffee no Coke, that's right. Doesn't do us any good at all.

CHRISTOPHER. Mm.

BRUCE. Gets us over excited.

CHRISTOPHER. Yeah yeah yeah yeah makes me jumpy.

BRUCE. That's right so — what shall we have instead?

CHRISTOPHER. I dunno.

BRUCE. What would you like?

CHRISTOPHER. What I'd really like is a Snakebite. D'you

6

know what I mean?

BRUCE. A Snakebite. Right, well —

CHRISTOPHER. Cider and Red Stripe or, you know, or a rum and black or or or …

BRUCE. Chris, Christopher … what's the rule on alcohol now?

CHRISTOPHER. But —

BRUCE. What's the rule on alcohol in here?

CHRISTOPHER. Alcohol. *(Pause.)* Oh yeah. Alcohol. Heh heh. D'you know what I mean?

BRUCE. What does alcohol do?

CHRISTOPHER. It makes your blood thin.

BRUCE. No … well possibly but —

CHRISTOPHER. Makes you see things.

BRUCE. Well … yes but —

CHRISTOPHER. See into the future maybe.

BRUCE. Well … s … sometimes maybe but what does it mostly do?

CHRISTOPHER. It fucks you up.

BRUCE. It fucks you up. Precisely. How about a glass of water. Eh? Some nice cool water? From the, from the thing?

CHRISTOPHER. Water from the thing. That's cool.

BRUCE. Nice cool water yes. Let me — just hold on … *(Bruce gets up and Christopher suddenly gets up too.)* No no — you're all right I'm just —

CHRISTOPHER. No you're all right —

BRUCE. *(Sitting.)* Help yourself —

CHRISTOPHER. *(Sitting.)* No no I'll —

BRUCE. I'll — look — this is silly. *(Bruce gestures.)*

CHRISTOPHER. Are you sure?

BRUCE. Be my guest. *(Christopher gets up and goes to the water cooler, takes two cups, pours.)* Sorted.

CHRISTOPHER. *(Drinking shakily.)* Sorted for E's and Whiz.

BRUCE. … Indeed.

CHRISTOPHER. Sorted innit. Sorted for E's and Whiz.

BRUCE. Absolutely.

CHRISTOPHER. *(Sitting.)* D'you know what I mean? Heh heh. *You* must know what I mean? Eh? Eh? *Doctor. (Christopher puts a cup of water in front of Bruce and sips his own.)* D'you know what

7

I mean?

BRUCE. Huh. Of course …

CHRISTOPHER. D'you know what I mean?

BRUCE. Well … *(Pause.)* No. I don't.

CHRISTOPHER. Yeah you do. *(Bruce sips his water.)* Where's the *drugs,* man?

BRUCE. … Oh the *drugs.* Of course …

CHRISTOPHER. It's all that innit. "Where's the drugs man? Oh man, these patients giving me massive big headache man, massive big headache, what have I got in my doctor's bag, gimme some smack, where's some smack? Where's the Tamazie Party? This bad nigga patient I got. This *bad nigga dude* I know. My God! I Can't Take The Pressure!" Innit? Innit. Go home to the old lady — "Aw I can't take the pressure. Oh no. I can't calm down. Oh no — yes — no — I can't shag until you gimme the smack darling!" D'you know what I mean? Ha ha ha ha ha. Oh no. Ha ha. It's all that. You with me? *(Pause.)*

BRUCE. Well …

CHRISTOPHER. Yeah yeah … go on! Typical white doctor. This is how *white* doctors speak: "Drugs? What drugs? No drugs for *you,* nigga. 'Cos you'll only enjoy them! These are my drugs … "

BRUCE. It's not quite like that.

CHRISTOPHER. Deny. It's all you doctors do! Deny, man.

BRUCE. Well, I don't think so really …

CHRISTOPHER. *(Sipping water shakily.)* Bullshit. Bullshit. Why else would you do it? Why else are you here?

BRUCE. Well, Christopher, why do you think you're here?

CHRISTOPHER. Eh?

BRUCE. Why are you here? Why do you think you're here?

CHRISTOPHER. Why am I here?

BRUCE. Yes. *(Pause.)*

CHRISTOPHER. I dunno.

BRUCE. And you've been here awhile now.

CHRISTOPHER. Yeah — yes I have … that's true.

BRUCE. Why do you think that is? If you'd just wanted drugs you wouldn't really be here would you? You'd be out there. Scoring off somebody and … going home. Wouldn't you? *(Pause.)* I know I would! Ha ha. Have a smoke. Watch the football. *(Pause.)* N'ha ha. *(Pause.)* No. Obviously. I'm not a drug user — OK? You know. But joking aside — it doesn't make sense that anybody would be here just for drugs as opposed to say, you know, out there *enjoying,* enjoying their drugs. Having some fun. D'you see what I mean? *(Pause.)* I mean, they are supposed to be *recreational. (Pause.)* So my point is — and this is one of the things I want to talk to you about today — you're here to get better, aren't you? Because you've been very poorly. Haven't you? *(Long pause.)*

CHRISTOPHER. I dunno.

BRUCE. Ah.

CHRISTOPHER. What's up? I'm going home. You should be happy.

BRUCE. Well, I'm not as happy as you.

CHRISTOPHER. I been saying all along, there's nothing wrong with me and now you agree with me and, I just, I just, I just … I'm going home. *(Pause.)* I don't know why I'm here. *(Pause.)* It's mad innit. It's bonkers. Mad shit. First thing I said when I arrived. When I first come in here. I had a look, I saw all the all the all the, you know, the others, the other geezers and I thought … Fuck this. My God! These people are insane! Ha ha ha ha ha … Get Me Outta Here —

BRUCE. Ha ha yes —

CHRISTOPHER. It's a *nut*house, man.

BRUCE. I grant you — indeed — there are a fair proportion —

CHRISTOPHER. A *fair proportion?* You're kidding me.

BRUCE. Of quite, quite —

CHRISTOPHER. They are NUTS!

BRUCE. … crazy people here … yes —

CHRISTOPHER. Crazies man! Radio Rental. Mad as monkeys.

BRUCE. People with — well — we don't actually use the term "crazy" …

CHRISTOPHER. You just said it.

BRUCE. I know I just said it but — I shouldn't have — I was — humouring — I was you know — it's a no no.

CHRISTOPHER. But you just said it.

BRUCE. I know but — you see my point?

CHRISTOPHER. You said it first.

BRUCE. OK look … there are things we … there are terms we use which people used to use all the time, terms which used to be

9

inoffensive but things are a bit different now. Certain words.

CHRISTOPHER. Certain words, what words?

BRUCE. Just ... terms which aren't even that offensive but —

CHRISTOPHER. Same as I say, what's offensive about it?

BRUCE. Well —

CHRISTOPHER. It's *true!*

BRUCE. It's not true ... it's — OK — it's not even that — it's just inaccurate. Some terms are just inaccurate. "Crazy" is one of them. It's just unhelpful. Woolly.

CHRISTOPHER. "Woolly." Oh. OK. I'm sorry.

BRUCE. For example, people used to say "schizophrenic" all the time. "Such and such is schizophrenic." Because it's two things at once. OK. Used to denote a divided agenda, a dual identity, the analogy of a split personality. Except we know now that schizophrenia doesn't mean that at all. Split personality? Meaningless. OK? So it's an unhelpful term. It's inaccurate. What we call a "misnomer." And this is a sensitive subject. We must think carefully, be *specific.* Because it's too ... you know — it's too serious. *(Pause.)* You were diagnosed with "Borderline Personality Disorder." What does this mean? *(Pause.)* Borderline Personality Disorder. OK? Key word — *Borderline.* Because, clinically speaking, you're on the *Border* between Neurotic and Psychotic.

CHRISTOPHER. Just ... on ... on ... on the border?

BRUCE. Yes. And that's a very useful term, isn't it? Because if people get the word wrong — if people just get the meaning of the word wrong, how can they get the person right? How can there be any ... any awareness. People don't know anything about it. They have stupid ideas. You lose out. So we try to "demystify." We try to explain. *(Pause.)* Which is what I wanted to talk to you about today. Your diagnosis. This term, this label, and what it means, because the thing is, I'm beginning to think, now ... it's ... well it's a little inaccurate —

CHRISTOPHER. YOU'VE MADE YOUR POINT I SAID I'M SORRY WHAT DO YOU WANT — BLOOD?

BRUCE. But I'm just saying ... in the light of recent developments —

CHRISTOPHER. Developments? What developments. What you on about, man? *(Robert, carrying a cup of coffee also in a plas-*

tic cup, appears at the door and just stands there waiting.)
ROBERT. You wanted to see me?
BRUCE. Doctor Smith. Yes come in. Hi.
ROBERT. How's tricks?
BRUCE. I'm fine. How are you?
ROBERT. I don't believe I've thanked you for that stupendous spread.
BRUCE. Sorry?
ROBERT. That succulent meal on Saturday. After the rugby. The food.
BRUCE. Oh. Thanks.
ROBERT. Hang onto that woman Bruce.
BRUCE. Sure.
ROBERT. You'll live to a hundred and three.
BRUCE. The thing is —
ROBERT. The only woman I know with the audacity to pull off a fondue. I thought, "Any minute now she'll be climbing into her caftan."
BRUCE. It was Welsh Rarebit.
ROBERT. Welsh Rarebit? The very thing.
BRUCE. I know it's not what you're used to —
ROBERT. On the contrary. It was just the ticket. Miserable and wet. Vanquished by The Frog and foot-sore.
BRUCE. Well, it soaked up the booze.
ROBERT. I couldn't believe that score. Not from The Frogs. Still, at least it wasn't Australia —
BRUCE. Doctor Smith —
ROBERT. Or New Zealand or any of the other hairy colonial outposts.
BRUCE. Doctor —
ROBERT. Welsh Rarebit eh? Took me back to my student days. Tie that woman to the nearest bed and inseminate her at once.
BRUCE. Doctor —
ROBERT. *Breed.* Lots of little Bruces. Have you thought any more about that loft conversion? All the rage when I was a student. Quite the thing for somebody in your circumstances. *(Robert winks at Christopher conspiratorially and Christopher just stares back blankly.)*

11

BRUCE. Doc —

ROBERT. That'll set you back a few quid. Still, when you become a consultant …

BRUCE. D —

ROBERT. That's where the big bucks are.

BRUCE. The thing is —

ROBERT. *(To Christopher.)* Hello.

BRUCE. You remember *Christopher?* Chris, do you remember Doctor Smith? Senior Consultant.

CHRISTOPHER. Warning warning warning! Alien life form approaching, Will Robinson.

ROBERT. Mm ha ha ha —

BRUCE. Mm yes —

ROBERT. Very witty —

BRUCE. OK … look —

CHRISTOPHER. Warning warning warning … d'you know what I mean?

BRUCE. Let's not get too distracted.

ROBERT. I'm distracting you of course.

BRUCE. No no you —

ROBERT. I —

BRUCE. I want you to —

ROBERT. Well of course you asked me to —

CHRISTOPHER. D'you know what I mean?

BRUCE. I've asked Doctor Smith to sit in today.

ROBERT. Yes that's right. Just got myself a nice cup of coffee and I'll just *lurk* in the corner …

CHRISTOPHER. *(Simultaneously with "corner.")* Coffee…!

ROBERT. You won't know I'm here.

CHRISTOPHER. He's got coffee.

BRUCE. There's plenty of water in the —

CHRISTOPHER. Oh wow!

BRUCE. That's not for you.

CHRISTOPHER. *(Reaching over and gesturing for coffee.)* Oh come on man. Coffee!

BRUCE. Chris … Chris … *(To Robert.)* Excuse me.

CHRISTOPHER. I want a cup of coffee.

BRUCE. Christopher hey listen, that's not yours.

CHRISTOPHER. I'll split it with you.

BRUCE. Is that yours or isn't it?

CHRISTOPHER. Come on man.

BRUCE. Chris … Chris come on! What's the rule on coffee? *(Christopher sits and kisses his teeth.)* No Coke no coffee. I'm sorry. You know why.

CHRISTOPHER. Why?

BRUCE. You know why.

CHRISTOPHER. Yeah but I get out tomorrow. I'm getting out.

ROBERT. I think your man has a point. *(Bruce looks at Robert. Robert takes out a packet of cigarettes and lights one.)* Sorry. I am distracting you. *(Robert gets up to leave but Bruce gestures for him to sit.)*

BRUCE. Please, you aren't. Really.

CHRISTOPHER. You got cigarettes! Gimme a cigarette doc, just one, I'm gagging for a puff, d'you know what I mean? *(Bruce nods. Robert sits again and offers the pack to Christopher who takes a cigarette, then another, then another two, putting one behind his ear, two in his top pocket and one in his mouth. Robert lights the cigarette for him and Christopher exhales a plume of smoke.)*

ROBERT. Better?

CHRISTOPHER. It's my nerves. I'm getting out tomorrow. You can't tell me what to do when I get out — when I'm out there — which is in *(Checks his watch.)* exactly twenty-four hours. I'm not under your … it's none of your business then man. I'm twenty-four hours away from freedom. Out of this hole. D'you know what I mean? *(Pause.)* Forty-eight hours tops.

ROBERT. Give him some coffee, he's going home. I haven't touched mine. *(Robert offers the coffee, Christopher reaches for it but Bruce is there first and takes the cup, drains it in one and throws it expertly into a waste-paper bin in the corner.)*

CHRISTOPHER. Hey man —

BRUCE. Coffee's got caffeine in it.

ROBERT. Or a nice cup of tea?

BRUCE. So has tea. The water's over there.

CHRISTOPHER. What did you do that for?

ROBERT. If this isn't a good time…?

BRUCE. No it's perfect timing. I wanted you to see this.

ROBERT. See what?

CHRISTOPHER. I'm already *packed.*

BRUCE. You're packed?

ROBERT. I'll just —

CHRISTOPHER. Yeah man. What you think I'm not in a *hurry? (To Robert.)* I could use a coffee to give me a bump. Just to get me on my way d'you know what I mean?

BRUCE. Who said you could pack?

ROBERT. *(Half standing, hovering.)* Look, I can just —

CHRISTOPHER. No one man, I just did it. I just, (no, you stay there) I put my pajamas in a bag and my toothbrush in on top. (Don't move) Took a whole five minutes. Shoot me. What, you think I "pinched the towels" and some stationery?

BRUCE. The thing is …

CHRISTOPHER. 'Cos I'm I'm I'm … I'm what?

ROBERT. I can come back —

CHRISTOPHER. Because I'm…? (No you're all right.) 'Cos I'm…?

BRUCE. No — I'm — No —

CHRISTOPHER. No what? You don't even know what I was gonna say. What was I gonna say?

ROBERT. Or I can stay?

BRUCE. No, no I wasn't —

CHRISTOPHER. Because I'm a Brother? *(Pause.)*

BRUCE. *(To Robert.)* Paranoia. Persecution Delusion —

CHRISTOPHER. 'Cos I'm an "uppity nigga."

BRUCE. No. You always say that and I always tell you the same thing. No.

ROBERT. I'll come back shall I?

BRUCE. Doctor Smith —

CHRISTOPHER. WOULD YOU JUST MAKE UP YOUR MIND BEFORE I GO STARK STARING BANANAS? Bouncing about like Zebedee.

BRUCE. Christopher —

CHRISTOPHER. Don't Christopher me man … (One sip of coffee he thinks he's Batman.)

BRUCE. You know that's not the way to talk to the Consultants.

CHRISTOPHER. He's giving me the fear.

BRUCE. Calm down. Now you are acting like a —

CHRISTOPHER. A what? A what. Go on say it. An "uppity nigga." *(Christopher kisses his teeth and starts eyeballing Robert.)*
BRUCE. Well … OK yes frankly you are and that's not what we do is it? Eh? And when you get out of here, if you start staring at people like that, what are they going to think?
CHRISTOPHER. What?
BRUCE. What are people going to think? When you get out? When you're ready…?
CHRISTOPHER. I don't fucking know.
BRUCE. Well what do you think they're gonna think?
CHRISTOPHER. I don't know.
BRUCE. They'll think you're a, a, an "uppity nigga," that's what they'll think. Kissing your teeth. It's not you. It's silly. It's *crazy.* You're not a, a, a, some type of "Yardie" —
CHRISTOPHER. Now you're telling me who I am?
BRUCE. No, I'm —
CHRISTOPHER. You're telling me who I am?
BRUCE. I'm telling you … to be You.
CHRISTOPHER. That's rum that is. That's rich. Now I've got an identity crisis. You're a cheeky fucking monkey you are. *(Pause.)*
ROBERT. Mm. "Uppity" isn't strictly speaking a term we —
BRUCE. *(To Robert.).* Learned Un-responsiveness? Disorganized Behaviour? Decline in Social Skills? Do you get me?
ROBERT. So?
BRUCE. Eh?
ROBERT. Look around you. *Who isn't* unresponsive, and disorganized with declining social skills? Eh? Heh heh. It's *normal.* *(Pause.)* Uh-huh huh huh.
BRUCE. Could we have a quiet word? *(Christopher stands abruptly and slams his fist on the desk.)*
CHRISTOPHER. Hey! You! I'm talking to you. When I get out of this place, people won't think *anything* because I'll be gone, Boy. I'm going far away where I can get some peace and quiet, no people, no cars, pollution, planes flying overhead like fruit flies, no cities, no fucking TV's, no construction work, no roadworks, no drills, no neighbours squatting on my head, under the floor, through the walls, rowing all day and night. Nothing. No people at all man and nobody looking at me funny like they never seen a

15

Brother before except on fucking *Sesame Street*! I'm going far away. (What's he looking at?) Look at you — nervous as a tomcat with big balls. D'you think I'm gonna eat you? I might do just to see the look on your face.

BRUCE. Nobody's looking at you funny Chris.

CHRISTOPHER. He is.

ROBERT. Well are you surprised?

CHRISTOPHER. What?

ROBERT. Are you surprised? Look at yourself. Now just … sit down and … relax would you? Of course people stare at you when you act like this. You know that, you know what it's like. *(Christopher looks from one to another, kisses his teeth. Pause.)*

BRUCE. *(To Robert.)* Overburdened Nervous System. Can't look me in the eye. Thinks we're staring at him.

ROBERT. We are. *(Pause.)*

CHRISTOPHER. I'm gone, oh yes. Believe. A place with a desert. And beaches. Palm trees. Somewhere hot. D'you know what I mean?

BRUCE. Chris…? Would you mind waiting in the other room for two minutes?

CHRISTOPHER. What did I say?

BRUCE. Nothing at all, we just need to —

ROBERT. Consult.

BRUCE. That's right.

ROBERT. That's why the badge says "Consultant." (I'm not wearing it.)

BRUCE. Please. I'd really appreciate it. Just go through that door.

CHRISTOPHER. *(Sighs.)* Okay. But I hope you know what you're doing, yeah?

BRUCE. How do you mean?

CHRISTOPHER. I hope you're not gonna let him talk you into anything.

ROBERT. Good god no. No no no no no.

CHRISTOPHER. Hope you're not gonna go changing your mind on me. 'Cos my twenty-eight …

BRUCE. Chris …

CHRISTOPHER. My twenty-eight days —

BRUCE. I know —

CHRISTOPHER. My twenty-eight days is up. It's up man. You've had your fun. I'm gone. Believe.

BRUCE. Uh-huh, OK … thank you. *(Christopher stands, lingers, stares at them both, then goes through a door. Silence.)* Do you think he knows?

ROBERT. What's there to know? He's a Section 2. His twenty-eight days are up. He's responded to treatment and now he's going home. *(Pause.)* Am I right?

BRUCE. But —

ROBERT. But what?

BRUCE. Well … I mean, you know what I'm going to ask you don't you? *(Pause.)*

ROBERT. What?

BRUCE. I want a Section 3.

ROBERT. Take a deep breath, and forget you even thought of it.

BRUCE. But —

ROBERT. Let him out. You're doing the right thing.

BRUCE. But I'm not.

ROBERT. Yes, this is right. You are doing what is fair and right and *just* and textbook medically beneficial. *(Pause.)* And apart from anything else we don't have the beds.

BRUCE. I'm really quite concerned —

ROBERT. Those beds are Prioritized for Emergency Admissions and Level Ones. Otherwise we'll wind up with a hospital full of long-term chronic mental patients hurtling about on *trolleys* — it'll be like *The Wacky Races*.

BRUCE. Look —

ROBERT. There'd be scandal. They'd have my arse out of here faster than his and you'd be next. That's right. I'll never make Professor. You'll never make your Specialist Registrar Training. What were we saying on Saturday?

BRUCE. When?

ROBERT. After the rugby. What did we talk about?

BRUCE. I dunno, what?

ROBERT. Well, your Specialist Registrar Training. And I said, for the coming year I am prepared to supervise you, I'll be your "Mentor," I'll teach you "all I know" … but you have to play the game.

17

BRUCE. "Play the game"?

ROBERT. That's right. I'll push your barrow. I'll feed the scrum but you're going to have to kick the ball into touch once in a while.

BRUCE. But —

ROBERT. But you can't afford to be indecisive about this.

BRUCE. But I *am* indecisive.

ROBERT. You can't afford not to follow my advice is what I mean.

BRUCE. Oh, that kind of indecisive.

ROBERT. They'll close the hospital down and build another Millennium Dome.

BRUCE. Nobody's going to close the hospital because of one Section 3. Are they? D'you think…?

ROBERT. Yes. Perhaps.

BRUCE Really?

ROBERT. Yes. Perhaps. *(Pause.)* Follow The Path Of Least Resistance.

BRUCE. But … I can't justify throwing him out on the basis of beds.

ROBERT. You're not "throwing him out" … you're doing what we are here to do. What *they* are here for us to do — and what everybody *expects* us to do. *(Pause.)* Eh? You are giving this man his *freedom.* You are releasing this man into the bosom of the community. You are giving him back his life. He's going back to his people.

BRUCE. His "people"? He doesn't have any *people.* He doesn't have a life.

ROBERT. That's a matter of conjecture.

BRUCE. It's true. He's on the White City Estate. It's a predominantly Jamaican community, he didn't grow up there, he doesn't know anybody and he hates it.

ROBERT. Where did he grow up?

BRUCE. All over the place. Peripatetic childhood.

ROBERT. What about family? He must have a mother.

BRUCE. He doesn't seem to be in contact with her anymore.

ROBERT. Are you proposing to Section this man *again* on the basis that he — what — he's lonely?

BRUCE. It'll do his head in.

ROBERT. It'll do his head in if you Section him again.

18

BRUCE. He isn't ready to go. You heard him. He's unstable.

ROBERT. Borderline Personality Disorder. On the border of neurotic and psychotic.

BRUCE. He was highly animated, shouting, staring.

ROBERT. You'd shout and stare if you were on the border of neurotic and psychotic.

BRUCE. The Loosening of Associations? The paranoia?

ROBERT. And you can add, reckless, impulsive, prone to extreme behavior, problems handling personal life, handling money, maintaining a home, family, sex, relationships, alcohol, a fundamental inability to handle practically everything that makes us human — and hey Some People Are Just Like That. Borderline. On the border. Occasionally visits but doesn't live there. See, technically he's not *that* mentally ill. We can't keep him here. It's Ugly but it's Right. *(Pause.)* Shoot me, those are the rules. *(Pause.)*

BRUCE. Christopher is Schizophrenic. *(Pause.)* Did you hear me?

ROBERT. No, he's BPD.

BRUCE. If you Section 3 him I can keep him here until he's properly diagnosed.

ROBERT. No. Absolutely not.

BRUCE. He's a Type 1 Schizophrenic with Positive Symptoms including Paranoid Tendencies. Probably Thought Disorder as well.

ROBERT. Is he delusional?

BRUCE. Sometimes.

ROBERT. How delusional?

BRUCE. Give me time and I'll show you.

ROBERT. You haven't got time. He's been here a month. He's been steadily improving — it's therefore a brief Psychotic Episode associated with BPD. Nothing more insidious.

BRUCE. He's Paranoid. You heard him.

ROBERT. How does BPD with Paranoia sound? Stick to the ICD 10 Classification.

BRUCE. You love the ICD 10 don't you? All the different euphemisms for "He's Nuts" without actually having to admit he's nuts. It's like your Linus blanket.

ROBERT. OK. BPD and A Bit Nuts.

BRUCE. No. Doctor. Please.

ROBERT. "Eccentric."

BRUCE. Look —

ROBERT. Was he squiffy?

BRUCE. ... "Squiffy"?

ROBERT. "Squiffy." Intoxicated. When he was Sectioned.

BRUCE. ... Yes ... I think ...

ROBERT. BPD with Alcoholism. It's a movable feast.

BRUCE. What? No it's not!

ROBERT. It's a matter of "opinion." And I'd be loath to re-Section the boy on the basis of a difference of opinion. It's semantics. And right now doctor, my semantics are better than yours so I win.

BRUCE. I can't live with that diagnosis. *(Pause.)*

ROBERT. But what's he done?

BRUCE. He hasn't done anything yet.

ROBERT. Has he tried to harm himself?

BRUCE. No.

ROBERT. Has he tried to harm anybody else?

BRUCE. Of course not.

ROBERT. Well you can't Section him again until he does something. Is he a danger to himself or to the public is what I'm getting at.

BRUCE. You want to wait until he becomes dangerous?

ROBERT. What's the Risk Factor? Come on. Write it down. Pretend you're running a business.

BRUCE. "Pretend I'm ... running a business"?

ROBERT. If we don't keep him in here — if we do not make this "very costly outlay ... "

BRUCE. Well it *is* risky.

ROBERT. How risky?

BRUCE. *Very* risky.

ROBERT. What did he do before?

BRUCE. Before when?

ROBERT. Before he was admitted. What happened?

BRUCE. He was ... he was in the market ... doing ... I dunno, something funny.

ROBERT. He was doing "something funny" in the market. Which market?

BRUCE. Does it matter?

ROBERT. I'm curious.

BRUCE. Shepherd's Bush.

ROBERT. "Funny" strange or "funny" ha-ha?

BRUCE. It's in the file. Read the file.

ROBERT. Why can't you just tell me?

BRUCE. I'd rather not.

ROBERT. Why not?

BRUCE. I'd just rather not. *(Pause.)*

ROBERT. Why not Doctor? What did he do?

BRUCE. It's rather delicate.

ROBERT. Well if you're going to be coy about it —

BRUCE. I just don't think it's relevant.

ROBERT. We can't keep him in here unless he's dangerous. You know the rules.

BRUCE. I think he's becoming depressed.

ROBERT. *I'm* becoming depressed now. *(Pause.)* Look. Doctor. If you keep him here long enough he won't be *able* to go home because he won't know what home *is* anymore.

BRUCE. OK. In a perfect world, forgetting about "resources," forgetting about "budgetary constraints" — say we've got *unlimited* beds — what would you do?

ROBERT. In a perfect world I'd send him home with fucking bells on and spread a little happiness. Why the hell not? Now, you have a job to do. If you don't feel you can do that job, you go away and have a think for a while. You know, in the medical wilderness, in your new job proof-reading for the fucking *Lancet* writing Bolshevik columns for *Welsh Doctor Weekly.* *(Pause.)* Is he still in there? Where is he?

BRUCE. He's in there.

ROBERT. In the … the …

BRUCE. That little room.

ROBERT. What little room? The cleaner's room?

BRUCE. No the, you know. That little waiting room. That's where they go to wait. It's a new thing. *(Pause.)*

ROBERT. You know, there is nothing wrong with your patient Bruce. He may be a bit jumpy, he may be a bit brusque, a bit shouty, a bit OTT — but hey, maybe that's just what you do where he comes from.

BRUCE. "Where he comes from"?

ROBERT. His "community."

BRUCE. He comes from Shepherd's Bush. What exactly are you trying to say?

ROBERT. I'm not saying anything.

BRUCE. "Where he comes from"? What are you saying?

ROBERT. I'm not saying anything.

BRUCE. Go on. What are you saying?

ROBERT. Nothing. *(Pause.)* I'm only saying. *(Pause.)* Maybe … maybe, maybe it's just you. Maybe you just make him nervous. Eh?

BRUCE. *What?*

ROBERT. Hear me out, it happens. This is the question we must ask ourselves. As a profession.

BRUCE. "Is it me? Do I just make him nervous?"

ROBERT. Yes.

BRUCE. He's a Paranoid Schizophrenic.

ROBERT. "Allegedly."

BRUCE. This is ridiculous.

ROBERT. We spend our lives asking whether or not this or that person is to be judged normal, a "Normal" person, a "Human," and we blithely assume that we know what "Normal" is. What "Human" is. Maybe he's more "Human" than us. Maybe *we're* the sick ones.

BRUCE. He's "more human than us"?

ROBERT. Yes.

BRUCE. And we're the sick ones.

ROBERT. Maybe. *(Pause.)*

BRUCE. *Why? (Silence.)*

ROBERT. OK, I'm being "whimsical." I'm being "capricious." But maybe, just maybe he's a right to be angry and paranoid and depressed and unstable. Maybe it's the only suitable response to the human condition?

BRUCE. What?

ROBERT. The human species is the only species which is innately insane. "Sanity is a conditioned response to environmental"…

BRUCE. I don't believe you're saying this …

ROBERT. … "stimulate." Maybe — just maybe it's true.

BRUCE. Maybe it's *utter horseshit. (Beat.)* I'm sorry. Doctor Smith. But. Which, which existential novelist said that? I mean, um, you'll be quoting R.D. Laing next.

ROBERT. That was R.D. Laing.

BRUCE. R.D. Laing was a *madman*. They don't come any fruitier.

ROBERT. I think there's something in it …

BRUCE. Should you be telling me this? Because, when I was at Med School, you know, this is not the sort of thing I learnt.

ROBERT. Well, with respect Doctor, maybe it's time you grew up, eh? Loosen up, calm down, get your head out of your textbooks and learn a little about *humanity*. Humanity Doctor. Being Human. As the poet said, Alan Ginsberg, *Alan Ginsberg* said this, I'll never forget it … "Human is not a noun, it's a *verb*." *(Pause.)* Eh? Don't be so *old-fashioned*. *(Silence.)*

BRUCE. Alan Ginsberg.

ROBERT. OK bad example. But listen … The Government guidelines clearly state that The Community is the preferred and proper place and it's my duty to subscribe to that. Otherwise it's no end of trouble.

BRUCE. If I let him out he will have a breakdown and succumb to all the most horrifying symptoms of Schizophrenia undiagnosed, unchecked, unsupervised and unmedicated.

ROBERT. Doctor Flaherty —

BRUCE. And we can't do anything about it —

ROBERT. Doctor Flaherty.

BRUCE. Because of policy?

ROBERT. Calm down.

BRUCE. I'm sorry. Um, you're right. I'm calm.

ROBERT. If you detain this man any longer he will become institutionalized. He won't get any better he'll get worse. You will make him ill. *(Pause.)*

BRUCE. Well, um I don't believe I will. *(Robert goes to the door, opens it. Christopher comes through the door.)*

ROBERT. You can come back in now. We've finished our little chat. Sit down, there's a good fellow. Can I get you anything, a cup of water? *(Robert pours another cup for Christopher, who drinks thirstily. Christopher paces a moment.)*

BRUCE. Thirsty? *(Christopher nods and holds his cup out for refill. He drinks it and goes back to pacing.)* That'll be the Haloperidol. Are you still stiff?

CHRISTOPHER. I'm jumping like a leaf. I been walking it off.

BRUCE. Try not to.

CHRISTOPHER. I like walking.

BRUCE. I know. And that's how you get lost.

CHRISTOPHER. I walked to the Hanger Lane Gyratory once.

ROBERT. Bravo.

BRUCE. No, not Bravo, you must try and control it.

ROBERT. Oh let him walk if he wants to walk. Goodness gracious. You go ahead and walk to Hanger Lane. Enjoy. Now. When were you planning on leaving us?

CHRISTOPHER. *(Pacing.)* Twenty-four hours.

ROBERT. Morning, evening?

CHRISTOPHER. After I've had my lunch.

ROBERT. And you have somewhere to go I take it.

BRUCE. Council Accommodation. White City.

ROBERT. Marvelous.

CHRISTOPHER. Only I don't go there.

ROBERT. Oh.

CHRISTOPHER. I don't like White City.

ROBERT. Why not?

CHRISTOPHER. 'Cos of the Fuzz.

ROBERT. The "fuzz."

CHRISTOPHER. The Filth. The Pigs. The Cops. The "Old Bill."

ROBERT. The police?

CHRISTOPHER. I get stopped a *lot* in White City. That's why I was arrested in Shepherd's Bush. 'Cos they all talk to each other on their walkie-talkies. They was waiting for me. They came to get me in the market. Come all the way from White City for me. Believe. I lost my shit

ROBERT. I see, well —

CHRISTOPHER. 'Cos they was after me, man.

ROBERT. And why do you think that is?

CHRISTOPHER. What? *Why?*

ROBERT. Yes, why? Why were they "after you"?

CHRISTOPHER. Why do you *think,* man?

ROBERT. I'm asking you.

CHRISTOPHER. 'Cos they're *fascists.* It's obvious. *(Silence.)*

ROBERT. Where would you like to live?

CHRISTOPHER. Where?

ROBERT. Would you prefer?

CHRISTOPHER. Africa.

ROBERT. Africa. *(Pause. Christopher sits and stares at Robert with intensity.)* A ha ha ha. Yes, very good. And why not?

CHRISTOPHER. I already told you.

ROBERT. Yes but I mean, for the time being.

CHRISTOPHER. There is no time being. I'm going to Africa. Central Africa. Where my dad come from.

ROBERT. Ah. Well … when you get out, if you, if things work out for you and you get a … have you got a job to go back to?

CHRISTOPHER. Got a job in Africa.

ROBERT. O … K … Somewhere to stay?

CHRISTOPHER. In Africa. In Uganda. *(Silence.)*

ROBERT. Friends?

CHRISTOPHER. In Africa.

ROBERT. *(Beat.)* Excellent. *(Robert stands.)* Well, I think I've pretty much finished here. Doctor Flaherty?

BRUCE. You're finished?

ROBERT. Quite finished. It's been nice chatting with you, Christopher. I sincerely hope I never clap eyes on you again, e-heh heh heh. *(Robert shakes Christopher's hand and Christopher just stares at him.)* It's a joke.

BRUCE. So you're going now?

ROBERT. Is that a problem? Unless you want me for anything else. *(They all look at each other. Christopher is still shaking Robert's hand.)*

CHRISTOPHER. *(To Robert.)* What's up with him? *(To Bruce.)* What's up your arse, man?

BRUCE. If you don't mind, I'd like you to stay while I ask Chris a couple more questions.

ROBERT. What sort of questions?

BRUCE. Routine. My assessment isn't over yet. *(Robert sits reluctantly, taking his hand back.)*

ROBERT. Why not? Fire away.

BRUCE. Because. The thing is Chris, Doctor Smith here says that you can go if you want to.

CHRISTOPHER. I know. I'm going.

BRUCE. But I'm wondering if you really want to?

CHRISTOPHER. I want it *bad*, d'you know what I mean?

BRUCE. And … you're *sure* you're ready. Are you sure?

CHRISTOPHER. I'm cool. *(Pause.)*

BRUCE. OK. Just a couple of questions.

CHRISTOPHER. Shoot.

BRUCE. What's in the fruit bowl?

CHRISTOPHER. How d'you mean?

BRUCE. What do you see in the fruit bowl? What type of fruit do you see? *(He proffers the bowl full of oranges. Christopher stares at it long and hard. Bruce takes an orange and hands it to Christopher who stares at it hard. He tosses one to Robert.)*

BRUCE. What's in the bowl, Chris?

CHRISTOPHER. Oranges.

BRUCE. Oranges, good, but what sort of oranges?

CHRISTOPHER. Just oranges.

BRUCE. Yes but they're not *orange* oranges, are they?

CHRISTOPHER. Nope.

BRUCE. What did you tell me yesterday? Can you remember? *(Pause.)*

CHRISTOPHER. They're Blue Oranges

BRUCE. Blue oranges. Really?

CHRISTOPHER. Bright blue.

BRUCE. Peel one. See what's inside. *(They wait as Christopher peels the orange, holds it up.)* What colour is it inside? *(Pause.)* Chris.

CHRISTOPHER. It's blue.

BRUCE. So the skin is blue — and even underneath the skin it's the same — it's blue?

CHRISTOPHER. That's correct. Completely blue. *(Pause.)* It's bad. It's a bad orange. Don't eat it. *(Pause.)* I mean, my God! Ha ha. What is it? "Black magic"?

BRUCE. Voodoo.

CHRISTOPHER. Voodoo! Oh no. *Spooky.* D'you know what I mean? It's — it's it's *nuts.*

BRUCE. "Spooky."

CHRISTOPHER. Spooky. "Yikes."

BRUCE. "Yikes" indeed …

CHRISTOPHER. "This bad nigga dude we got doing his voodoo again." My dad, right, my dad, that's his favorite fruit. Oranges.

Orange oranges, though. D'you know what I mean?

BRUCE. Who is your father Chris? Chris? *(Pause. Christopher eats a segment of orange.)* Who is your father?

CHRISTOPHER. How d'you mean?

BRUCE. What's his name?

CHRISTOPHER. I already told you.

BRUCE. Tell me again. In front of Robert.

CHRISTOPHER. Why?

BRUCE. Just … please Chris … it's a simple question.

CHRISTOPHER. It's difficult to answer. D'you know what I mean?

BRUCE. No I don't, why?

CHRISTOPHER. If I ask you who your father is nobody gives a shit. With me it's front-page news. D'you understand?

BRUCE. No, I don't understand. Why is it front-page news?

CHRISTOPHER. 'Cos of who he is.

ROBERT. Who is he?

CHRISTOPHER. I'm not telling you.

BRUCE. (This is ridiculous.) Look. Please. Help me out here.

CHRISTOPHER. You want *me* to help *you*? Now you want me to do your job.

ROBERT. If you can't tell us who he is — it'll be tricky for us to send you home. You will have to stay here. Do you understand?

BRUCE. Who's your father Chris? *(Pause.)*

CHRISTOPHER. It sounds silly.

BRUCE. For Christ's sake —

CHRISTOPHER. It's embarrassing.

BRUCE. Chris!

CHRISTOPHER. How can I say it, in all honesty, without you thinking I'm off the stick? How do I know it won't incriminate me, d'you know what I'm saying?

ROBERT. It won't incriminate you. We promise.

CHRISTOPHER. Oh you "promise"? Well in that case, I feel a whole lot better.

BRUCE. Please … just do this one thing for me. For me. *(Pause.)*

CHRISTOPHER. My father … my dad … was a very important man. Believe it or not … my dad … is former Ugandan President His Excellency Idi Amin.

BRUCE. Fabulous —

CHRISTOPHER. And if he knew I was here right now I would not want to be you.

BRUCE. Y-Chris —

CHRISTOPHER. I would not want to be you. Because The Man Does Not Fuck About, d'you understand what I'm saying? He will *digest* you. He will juice you and squirt you out of his arse like a motherfucking fire hose, into the sewers for the bats and fish. They don't call him "The Butcher of the Bush" for nothing. Believe. *(Silence.)*

ROBERT. Fine ... OK ...

CHRISTOPHER. What else d'you want to know?

ROBERT. Well —

CHRISTOPHER. He got forty-three children and a hundred grandchildren. He's a family man. He's a Muslim. He lives in Saudi Arabia. In exile. 'Cept when he goes on holiday to Paris. Every day he takes a delivery of East African oranges from the airport. Reminds him of the old times. He drives a Chevrolet and has a talent for the accordion. A lot of exiles drive Mercedes, but he don't like to draw attention to his self.

ROBERT. I see ...

CHRISTOPHER. He kicked my mum out of Uganda 'cos she's from Zaire. He kicked out all the foreigners. D'you know what I mean? I'm not proud of it. It's just the way he was. Old fashioned. *(Pause.)*

ROBERT. "Old ... fashioned." Mm ... *(Pause.)* Your mother is from Zaire, you say?

CHRISTOPHER. You don't believe me, do you?

ROBERT. When was this?

CHRISTOPHER. 1974. Before I was born.

ROBERT. *Before* you were born?

CHRISTOPHER. I was *conceived.* That's why she had to go. He couldn't father a foreigner. It's obvious. *(Bruce and Robert stare at each other.)* He's got another wife in Haringay who runs a chippie. Got closed down for bad hygiene, d'you know what I mean?

BRUCE. You can go back to your ward now. Chris? I'll see you later.

CHRISTOPHER. But —

BRUCE. It's over now.

CHRISTOPHER. We're finished?

BRUCE. We're finished for today, yes.

CHRISTOPHER. What did I say?

ROBERT. Absolutely nothing.

CHRISTOPHER. Did I pass? *(Bruce just smiles.)* Now you're not saying anything. That's no good.

BRUCE. You have nothing to worry about.

CHRISTOPHER. I don't, yeah?

BRUCE. No. You're going to be fine.

CHRISTOPHER. I'm still going home, right? *(Pause.)* I'm still going home, yeah? *(Pause.)* I'm … I'm still going home?

ROBERT. Shhh … OK? Just relax. *(Pause.)*

CHRISTOPHER. But … I'm —

ROBERT. Shhh. *(Pause.)*

CHRISTOPHER. I'm —

ROBERT. *(Waving a finger.)* Uh. Uh-uh. *(Pause.)*

CHRISTOPHER. But I'm still going home aren't I?

ROBERT. Of course you are.

BRUCE. Chris? I'll speak to you later. Go back to your ward now.

CHRISTOPHER. But I'm still going home, yeah?

ROBERT. Yes. *(Bruce takes back the remains of the orange. Christopher gets up and shuffles out. Robert takes the remains of the orange from Bruce and eats a segment.)*

ROBERT. Very interesting.

BRUCE. Happy?

ROBERT. "Le Monde Est Bleu Comme Une Orange."

BRUCE. What?

ROBERT. It's a poem by Paul Éluard. He was a French Surrealist.

BRUCE. You don't say.

ROBERT. The World Is As Blue As An Orange. *(Beat.)* It's an analogy.

BRUCE. Classic hallucinatory behaviour.

ROBERT. Or is it a simile?

BRUCE. Already he's building a system of logic around it … his "father" who loves oranges de da de da de da.

ROBERT. Hypomania. Brief psychotic episode requiring short-term hospital treatment and a course of antipsychotics when he goes home. Simple.

BRUCE. What if it isn't? What if it's just the tip of the iceberg?

ROBERT. Is he hearing voices? Auditory hallucinations?

BRUCE. Not yet.

ROBERT. Is he seeing other things — other than blue oranges?

BRUCE. Isn't this enough?

ROBERT *(Shrugs.)* For some reason he wants to see blue instead of orange. Neurotics do it all the time. They see what they want to see, not what they really see. Maybe he knows the poem.

BRUCE. You're joking, aren't you?

ROBERT. Entirely serious. There's a lot of French speakers in Central Africa. His mother could have read it him as a child. It planted an image in his mind. When he's not a hundred percent that image presents itself.

BRUCE. You are joking.

ROBERT. There's a Tin-Tin book. *Tin-Tin and the Blue Oranges.* It's about a "mad professor" who invents an orange which will grow in the Sahara. Only trouble is it's bright blue and tastes salty. Tin-Tin was banned in the Belgium Congo. They thought he was a communist. But in colonial Uganda the notoriety no doubt made Tin-Tin a "must read" for the bourgeoisie. He was a cultural icon and a symbol of middle class insurrection. A delusion waiting to happen. BPD with Delusion.

BRUCE. Are you making this up? *(Robert shakes his head.)* Surely, you must agree, there's something terribly wrong here. Surely we have a Responsibility to …

ROBERT. A Responsibility to let him out. Level 2. Prescribe medication, CPN twice weekly.

BRUCE. He won't take medication, you know that, they never do.

ROBERT. That's what we have CPN's for. Just till he's back on his feet.

BRUCE. They never do because it's dated toxic crud which will paralyse him from the skull downwards and make his life a misery.

ROBERT. Precisely.

BRUCE. So…?

ROBERT. New generation antipsychotics. Clozapine, Risperidone, Olanzapine. Let him go home.

BRUCE. He needs looking after.

ROBERT. Maybe he does, maybe he doesn't. Maybe he really does have some connection with Idi Amin. Jesus-Christ-on-a-mountain-bike. The man was spawning offspring all over the shop.

BRUCE. You can't be serious.

ROBERT. Maybe I am.

BRUCE. Oh for God's sake!

ROBERT. OK, calm down. *(He paces and wipes his hands on his shirt, rubs his hands together, talks with a mouthful.)* Now, *(Clears his throat.)* for what it's worth, it's quite possible he's heard some family story, handed down through the generations, some apocryphal story, maybe Idi Amin came to town, to the village, de da de da, Chinese whispers, it's just gathered importance, gained in stature and now he believes this. It happens. Read my manuscript.

BRUCE. What manuscript?

ROBERT. It's a continuation of my Ph.D. really. It's not finished. There's a chapter missing — something rather complex and enigmatic — a certain "je ne sais quoi." Seriously. I think there's something in it.

BRUCE. I think there's something in Feng Shui, Doctor, but I wouldn't do a Ph.D. in it.

ROBERT. As your Supervisor I wouldn't have it any other way.

BRUCE. You're saying he's not sick, it's a cultural thing.

ROBERT. I'm saying he's not mad. There's a difference. *(Pause.)* Do you know what happened to his mother in Uganda? Do you know whether she was raped by soldiers after the military coup? By Idi Amin himself? She could have been a journalist or a cook at State House for all you know. Have you asked her?

BRUCE. That's not possible.

ROBERT. Why not?

BRUCE. I can't trace her. We think she lives in Feltham.

ROBERT. Where in Feltham?

BRUCE. Nobody seems to have an address.

ROBERT. Find her. It might not *all* be true — but then again it might. Can you imagine the ramifications of that? This is precisely what I am getting at in my research.

BRUCE. What are you talking about? You can't use him for research.

ROBERT. Why not? Why ever not? Think about it. There is more mental illness amongst the Afro-Caribbean population in London than in any other ethnic grouping. Why? Is it the way we

31

are diagnosing it. Is it us? Is it them? What's causing it? What's the answer? What's the cure? There's no "cure" for Schizophrenia. No "cure" for Psychosis. Only *Palliative Drugs.* But what if it isn't Psychosis? Wouldn't that be a relief? What if there is a cure? Cognitive therapy. *Minimal* medication. A "cure" for "black psychosis." Imagine it. The Holy Grail. And imagine if the fucker who found it was … *us. (Silence.)*

BRUCE. "A Cure For Black Psychosis."

ROBERT. Figuratively speaking.

BRUCE. You're being "whimsical" again?

ROBERT. *(Shaking his head.)* An end to Palliatives. No more "dated toxic crud."

BRUCE. OK. Say it is true. It's all true. Christopher is Idi Amin's son. *And* he's a Schizophrenic. It's both. Had you thought of that? *(Pause.)* Kind of blows your theory out of the water, doesn't it? *(Silence.)*

ROBERT. OK look. I'm merely pointing out that sometimes our analysis is *Ethnocentric.* In this case you are evaluating the situation according to your own specific cultural criteria.

BRUCE. "Ethnocentric"?

ROBERT. Our Colonial Antecedents are latent and barely suppressed. We are intuitively suspicious because of *our* cultural background. For example, on the way back from the rugby the other night we stopped at the off-license for a bottle of wine. I noticed that the Hindu gentleman behind the counter said neither Please nor Thank You. I had to ask myself, is he just *like* that — or is he just *rude?* Or is it because there is no such thing as Please and Thank You in Hindi — is it not customary in his culture?

BRUCE. What are you talking about? He always says Please and Thank You.

ROBERT. OK fine. So perhaps I should ask myself, Is it me? What are my cultural expectations?

BRUCE. Look, after the rugby, everyone goes in there, all the rugger buggers, pissy drunk and *they* don't say please and thank you —

ROBERT. Nevertheless, we must guard against our Ethnocentricity.

BRUCE. I don't think I like the direction this is heading.

ROBERT. The point is, this is my *Province,* Doctor. That's why you asked me here. Because I know how many beans make five. I

am, as they say, an "expert." I am Senior Consultant and I am here to be "consulted." I am not here to be "bounced off." To "run it up the flagpole and see who salutes." I'm here because "I know."
BRUCE. But ... with the greatest respect Doctor Smith, you don't. He's *my* patient ... so ... really ...
ROBERT. OK fine. Whatever. Discharge him. Next case. *(Pause.)*
BRUCE. But —
ROBERT. We can skin this cat as artfully as we like, however, in the opinion of this highly experienced Department Head, Doctor Flaherty, what we have here is No Beds and, more importantly, a patient who has No Need Of A Bed.
BRUCE. But I think —
ROBERT. What I "think" is that you think too much. What I think is that you should let me do the thinking. Now if you don't mind, I'm very busy. *(Robert goes to the door.)*
BRUCE. But ... you're saying ... what you're really saying is that Christopher's ... unable to distinguish between realistic and utterly unrealistic notions because ... what...? Because he's...?
ROBERT. BPD. Case closed.
BRUCE. It's because he's b —
ROBERT. BPD. Goodbye doctor.
BRUCE. Because he's black? *(Robert sighs, clenches his teeth. Walks back into the room.)*
ROBERT. *(Icily.)* I'm saying where he comes from it is almost certainly not an unrealistic notion. Where we come from, it evidently is. Get it?
BRUCE. But he comes from Shepherd's Bush.
ROBERT. He sees himself as African. And we don't say "black" anymore —
BRUCE. Yes we do —
ROBERT. We say "African-Caribbean."
BRUCE. Where does the Caribbean come into it?
ROBERT. All right, he's "African."
BRUCE. From Shepherd's Bush.
ROBERT. I'm not going to quibble over this twaddle.
BRUCE. "Twaddle"?
ROBERT. I'm not going to squabble. His "origins" are in Africa.
BRUCE. How far back are you going?

ROBERT. And for the last time I'll remind you that you are under my Supervision, you are my subordinate, and your tone is beginning to sound dangerously insubordinate if not nakedly insulting.

BRUCE. I'm sorry ... but —

ROBERT. Do you know what most young doctors would do to have me as Supervisor? I mean normal ones ... the smart ones ... what they'd do to know they have a future. To have a shot at becoming Consultant? They'd *lick my anus. (Silence.)* (But that's beside the point ...) *(He goes to the door and looks out. Comes back. Sits.)* Now do you want me to recommend your Consultancy at this hospital or don't you?

BRUCE. Of course.

ROBERT. Then act like a professional. Act like a representative of the Royal College of Psychiatrists.

BRUCE. But I'm *not* a —

ROBERT. Do you want to be? Mm? Now. Pull yourself together. Try not to be so wet behind the ears. Otherwise I'm taking you off this case.

BRUCE. You can't take me off this case.

ROBERT. I'll assign a CPN and discharge him myself.

BRUCE. If you do I'll appeal to the Authority.

ROBERT. I am the Authority. (Just between you and me.) *(Pause.)*

BRUCE. But ... um ... with respect, it's it's it's it's what I believe in.

ROBERT. Well, you know, Doctor, with respect, that isn't good enough.

BRUCE. It's not good enough to do what I believe is right?

ROBERT. That's right. It's naive.

BRUCE. Naive?

ROBERT. That's right. You're naive. And you're beginning to get on my *wick. (Silence.)*

BRUCE. Why won't you listen to me?

ROBERT. What? "Listen to you"? To *you?* It's not my job to listen to you. It's *your* job to listen to ... oh for goodness sake ... *(Pause.)* OK. All right. Listen. Let me join up some of the dots for you. Let me do some of the math for you: Schizophrenia is the worst pariah. One of the last great taboos. People don't understand it. They don't want to understand it. It scares them. It depresses them. It is not treated with some glamorous and intriguing wonderdrug like

34

Prozac or Viagra. It isn't newsworthy. It isn't curable. It isn't heroine or Ecstasy. It is not the preserve of rock stars and super models and hip young authors. It is not a topic of dinner conversation. *Organized crime* gets better press. They make *movies* about junkies and alcoholics and gangsters and men who drink too much, fall over and beat their woman until bubbles come out of her nose but Schizophrenia my friend is just not in the phone book.

BRUCE. Then we must change that.

ROBERT. ... and then ... *what?*

BRUCE. Then we must change that.

ROBERT. "Change." Hmm. Well ... the thing is, you can't change that. D'you see? I can't. Seriously. The Authority — the rest of the Board, not even me — they will question your expertise. They will wonder why you got so upset about it. They will wonder whether this case has a "deeper personal significance" to you and they will undermine you at every turn and then they will screw you. As sure as eggs are fucking eggs.

BRUCE. A deeper personal...?

ROBERT. People will question your mental wellness. *(Silence.)* They'll say you are Mad. And then they'll say *I'm* Mad for Supervising you and allowing my department to disintegrate so.

BRUCE. Well if you don't want to Supervise me ... if you've changed your mind ... you only have to say.

ROBERT. Not at all. This is a "Teaching Hospital" and I am here to teach.

BRUCE. W ... was it Saturday? Did I say something after the rugby?

ROBERT. Look. I'm not the big bad wolf I'm not trying to undermine your decision and I certainly don't want to release Christopher if he isn't ready. I care. And I know you care. All I'm saying is that one can care too much. One can have too much Empathy — Understanding — an overweening Compassion. You try to be all things to all men: Doctor. Friend. A reasonable man. We all want to be reasonable men. Eh? Bruce? Please. Now. Am I not your friend? *(Pause.)* Aren't we friends? *(Bruce slowly nods.)*

ROBERT. Sleep on it. Let me conduct my own assessment. We can reconvene in the morning and decide together. Eh? I'll talk to him tonight. I promise you I won't be partisan.

BRUCE. OK. Fine. Whatever you say.

ROBERT. Don't look so gloomy. Just wait till you're a Consultant. Think of that loft conversion.

BRUCE. Robert ...

ROBERT. Bruce ... Bruce ... Bruce ... You have it all to look forward to. Trust me. I want what you want. I really do. I believe in what you believe in. I'm on your side. *(Blackout.)*

ACT TWO

That night. Robert and Christopher sit facing each other across the table. A reading light is the only light. Robert takes a cigarette from his pack and lights it. Christopher takes a cigarette from behind his ear and Robert lights it. They exhale.

ROBERT. Listen listen listen listen. *(Pause.)* Listen. *(Pause.)* We all have these thoughts. It's perfectly natural. Even I have them. Yes. Me. Some days I get home from work, from a long night in the hospital, visiting, ward rounds, nothing untoward, nothing terrible, a few cross words with a colleague, some silly argument, I get home and I get in the door and I slump. All the life drains out of me. I think ... Why Am I Doing This? Eh? What's in it for me? A table at The Ivy if I use the right prefix. A seminar in Norway. Some spotty young Registrar takes me to the rugby and hangs on my every word. Big deal. And there are times, when I look across at this Professor and that Professor turning up to work in a new Jag, he's just come back from La Rochelle, he's off to play a round of golf at his thousand pound a year golf club, have a drink at his jolly old Mayfair club, posh dinners with drug company reps, knighthoods, appearances on Radio Four n'ha ha ha ... And I think ... How do they do that? What, are they "experts" or something? I Want To Be Professor! What do they do that I don't? And the answer is: Who Cares? That's their life. Nevertheless, I feel small and I think my life adds up to nothing. And I have to keep reminding myself: Why not? Why not think these things? It's not greedy, it's not Covetous. It's human. It's me being a human being. And it applies to us all. And it's my right to do something about it. It's everybody's right to take steps. But *Killing Yourself?* Christopher? Why? *(Silence.)* Everybody Feels Like This. At some point. In their life. Everybody feels that they've ... lost out. It's The Human Condition. The capacity to feel *Disappointment.* It's

37

what distinguishes us from the animals. Our *disappointment.* Mm. It's true. The capacity to grieve for lost opportunity. For the lives we *could* have led. The men and women we *may* have become. It has us in an appalling stranglehold. And sometimes we say, Why Go On? And we want to end it all. The hell with it. Life's a sham. *That's* human too. You don't hear doggies running about going, "Oh that this too too solid flesh could melt." Of course not. Why not? They're *dogs!* It would be ridiculous. Dogs have other talents. They can lick their own balls. A talent for simplicity. N'ha ha ha. Do you see? Learn to cultivate a Talent For Simplicity. *(Pause.)*
CHRISTOPHER.   Learn To Lick My Balls? That's your expert advice, yeah?
ROBERT.   N'ha ha ha. N'ha ha ha well … it might work …
CHRISTOPHER.   You're a fucking *doctor,* man.
ROBERT.   I know, I'm joking but you, you, you see my point. This life is a *gift.* The food we eat, the smells we smell, the trees, the sky, the *fecundity* of Creation … it's a *really lovely* gift, and if for whatever reason you cannot see that right now, then I'm here to Heal Your Vision. To help you See. I promise you, I plead with you, I *entreat* you. Take a few deep breaths. Calm down. Think about this. You're not "Suicidal." It's ridiculous. *(Silence.)*
CHRISTOPHER.   I don't want to go home. *(Pause.)* I changed my mind. I'm not going.
ROBERT.   Christopher …
CHRISTOPHER.   I … I … I don't have a home. I'm not … I'm not ready.
ROBERT.   What happens to you when you go home?
CHRISTOPHER.   I told you about The Fuzz.
ROBERT.   OK. Fine. But apart from … the "fuzz." What else happens to you? *(Pause.)* Chris? *(Pause.)*
CHRISTOPHER.   People stare at me. Like they *know* … like they know about me. Like they know something about me that I don't know.
ROBERT.   Such as?
CHRISTOPHER.   Eh?
ROBERT.   What could they know that you don't know?
CHRISTOPHER.   I don't know. They hate me. They think I'm bad.
ROBERT.   Which people?

38

CHRISTOPHER. Eh?

ROBERT. Who are these people who … think you're bad?

CHRISTOPHER. I hear noises. At night. Outside my window. Sometimes I hear … talking. People talking about me.

ROBERT. Talking about you?

CHRISTOPHER. Laughing sometimes.

ROBERT. And you've no idea who it is?

CHRISTOPHER. No idea. Sometimes I hear machinery. Whirring. Like a … a strange droning noise. And beeping. A strange Beeping noise. Very loud.

ROBERT. It's the dustbin men.

CHRISTOPHER. On Saturdays and Sundays?

ROBERT. Builders. OK? We're in the midst of a property boom. Interest rates are low, people are buying and building and renovating — people want more of the life gifted them. Life is Rich. People are greedy for Life.

CHRISTOPHER. Not in White City they're not. "White City." "South Africa Road." Even the names are a fucking wind up.

ROBERT. But you have your friends. Your *community*. People who *care*.

CHRISTOPHER. I don't have any friends. I try to make friends with people but it's not easy. I try to make conversation but it's not easy. Sometimes I say the wrong thing. Actually I always say the wrong thing. I don't have a girlfriend. Who'd want me? *(Pause.)*

ROBERT. Well. You'll make new friends when you get out.

CHRISTOPHER. I made friends with Bruce.

ROBERT. You won't be alone in all this. I'll make sure of that.

CHRISTOPHER. Yeah but I want double-glazing. Don't talk to me about the fucking property boom. It's like living in a biscuit tin. *(Pause.)*

ROBERT. Well, you know, Chris, I can't provide you with double-glazing. It's not part of my remit. If you want double-glazing … Go to the Council. See your housing officer.

CHRISTOPHER. You said you would help me.

ROBERT. I know but —

CHRISTOPHER. So help me —

ROBERT. It's —

CHRISTOPHER. Help me —

ROBERT. It's not my job! N'ha ha ha. D'you see?

CHRISTOPHER. Yeah, but what I thought was, if I moved somewhere else —

ROBERT. OK. There's a procedure for that. The Council will have a procedure for transferring you.

CHRISTOPHER. Yeah but I wanna go to Africa.

ROBERT. You want to go to Africa.

CHRISTOPHER. I want to go to Africa.

ROBERT. Back to your roots.

CHRISTOPHER. My "roots"?

ROBERT. You feel you "belong" there?

CHRISTOPHER. *No,* man. I already told you. It's *nice* there. And and and you know I told you about my dad.

ROBERT. Idi Amin.

CHRISTOPHER. Idi Amin Dada. That's his proper name. Idi Amin Dada.

ROBERT. O … K … *(Pause.)* Tell me about your mother. What did she do in Uganda?

CHRISTOPHER. She was a barmaid.

ROBERT. A "barmaid." Really? In a pub?

CHRISTOPHER. No, in a shoe shop, innit.

ROBERT. Where the soldiers drank?

CHRISTOPHER. Eh?

ROBERT. Did many soldiers drink there?

CHRISTOPHER. I don't know.

ROBERT. What I'm getting at is … how … how did your mum actually meet President Amin? *(Silence. Christopher stares into space.)* Christopher?

CHRISTOPHER. You wouldn't understand.

ROBERT. Why wouldn't I understand?

CHRISTOPHER. You wouldn't understand. *(Silence.)*

ROBERT. Try me.

CHRISTOPHER. She was a student. He closed down the University for political reasons.

ROBERT. She told you this?

CHRISTOPHER. She never talks about it — d'you know what I mean? It's personal. *(Pause.)* She gets upset.

ROBERT. What did she read?

CHRISTOPHER. How d'you mean?

ROBERT. What was her subject? English Literature?

CHRISTOPHER. How d'you mean?

ROBERT. What I'm getting at is, well, does she read you poetry for example?

CHRISTOPHER. No.

ROBERT. What about at school? Did you read poetry at school?

CHRISTOPHER. No.

ROBERT. Oh. OK. Fine. *(Pause.)* What about books? Children's books? Comics? Tin-Tin? Asterix? She must have given you books.

CHRISTOPHER. No.

ROBERT. Do you still see her? Christopher? D'you know where she lives? *(Pause.)* Chris?

CHRISTOPHER. She lives in Feltham.

ROBERT. Do you know her address? Do you want to tell me? *(Pause.)* You don't want to tell me where she lives? Why should I believe you if you can't even tell me your mother's address?

CHRISTOPHER. Bruce don't believe me either but I can prove it.

ROBERT. You can "prove it"?

CHRISTOPHER. Yeah man.

ROBERT. How?

CHRISTOPHER. Why should I tell you?

ROBERT. Well … because I'm asking you to …

CHRISTOPHER. What if I don't trust you?

ROBERT. Well … then … that would be a great shame.

CHRISTOPHER. A shame? *(Beat.)* You think it'd be a shame, yeah?

ROBERT. Yeah.

CHRISTOPHER. Oh. *(Christopher weighs it up. He produces a wallet from his pocket, from the wallet he produces a tightly folded-up newspaper article. He unfolds it and holds it out to Robert. Robert hesitates, then takes it and reads. Christopher reads over his shoulder.)*

ROBERT. *(Reading.)* "A delivery of East African oranges from the airport … the Butcher of the Bush … talent for the accordion blah blah blah … Forty-three children by four wives … "

CHRISTOPHER. Five wives.

ROBERT. Eh?

CHRISTOPHER. Five wives really. There's a fifth. A *secret* one.

ROBERT. A … a … where?

41

CHRISTOPHER. *(Pointing.)* Not the one who runs a take-away. Another one. Common-law wife. Living in "penury."

ROBERT. *(Reading.)* "Living in ... in Feltham."

CHRISTOPHER. In "penury."

ROBERT. "In penury ... in Feltham." Bugger me. How long have you had this?

CHRISTOPHER. My mother gave it to me.

ROBERT. Bugger me. *(They look at each other. Silence.)*

CHRISTOPHER. *(Pointing.)* Look. That's his photo.

ROBERT. *(Holding the article.)* Can I keep this?

CHRISTOPHER. No you cannot keep that.

ROBERT. Please. Christopher ... listen ... *(Christopher snatches the article back, folds it, puts it away as he speaks.)*

CHRISTOPHER. I am being *harassed*. I'm in fear of my *life*. I live in *fear*. They Know Who I Am.

ROBERT. Who does?

CHRISTOPHER. The men. Where I live. The noises. The ... the *police. Work* men ... *police* men.

ROBERT. They're ... look ... it's ... they're just ordinary *men. Work* men ... *police* men.

CHRISTOPHER. Other men too. Another man. He throws bananas at me.

ROBERT. Bananas...?

CHRISTOPHER. When I'm at work. Even at work — d'you know what I mean! Big bloke with a little pointy head. Long thin arms trailing along the ground. A real knuckle-dragger. Very white skin. Hideous-looking bastard. He's the ringleader. I see him at night. He bangs on my door. Says he's coming to get me. He says he'll do me and nobody would even notice and I believe him. There's a whole family of them. A tribe. I don't like them at all. They're a race apart. *Zombies! The undead.* Monsters! Manchester United fans. *(Pause.)*

ROBERT. Football hooligans?

CHRISTOPHER. On Saturdays, I see 'em in the crowds at Loftus Road. They come after the game. And before the game. With bananas. With ... with shit smeared through the letterbox, not dog shit — real shit. Pissing through the letterbox, fires, firestarting on the front step. It's a disgrace. They call me "Jungle

Boy." If my dad was here he'd kill them dead. He'd monster them. Believe. *(Silence.)* It's their appearance that spooks me the most. Those tiny, bony, shrunken heads. All shaved. Ugly.

ROBERT. D'you mean ... Skinheads?

CHRISTOPHER. *Zombies.*

ROBERT. What makes you think these people are ... "The undead"?

CHRISTOPHER. They look *half* dead. It's that ghostly white skin, looks like tapioca, d'you know what I mean?

ROBERT. Christopher —

CHRISTOPHER. Baldies. "Baldy-heads," that's what I call them. Baldy-heads.

ROBERT. "Baldy-heads." I see. But ... they're not really ... "Zombies," now are they? Chris? Which is it, "Zombies," or "Baldy-Heads"? *(Pause.)* There is a difference.

CHRISTOPHER. D'you think it's funny?

ROBERT. Not in the least. It could be the difference between you staying here or you going home.

CHRISTOPHER. They're *dangerous,* man. Believe. They're spooky. I could be dead tomorrow. *(Robert rubs his eyes and sighs.)* You know the average life expectancy of the modern black male? Sixty-four years old. That's how long we got. What age do we get the Pension? *Sixty-five!* It's a fucking *ripoff,* man! D'you know what I mean?

ROBERT. So ... fundamentally, you don't think you're sick? Am I right?

CHRISTOPHER. Yeah I'm sick. Sick and *tired,* man. Sick of everything. I got problems. D'you know what I'm saying?

ROBERT. Do you keep a diary?

CHRISTOPHER. A diary? No. Do you?

ROBERT. You should start keeping a diary.

CHRISTOPHER. I never go out.

ROBERT. No, a diary of what *happens.*

CHRISTOPHER. Nothing ever happens, man. All day everything, nothing.

ROBERT. I meant, things on the estate. Concerning the letter-box...? OK? Then you go to the Council, you ask to see your housing officer and you show her the diary. She can have you transferred to a different estate.

43

CHRISTOPHER. It gets a bit lonely sometimes but

ROBERT. Yes I know and that's OK. That's normal. That's human. And I'll tell you something else —

CHRISTOPHER. Sometimes people scare me.

ROBERT. I know they do. And you know what you do when they do these things?

CHRISTOPHER. What?

ROBERT. You laugh.

CHRISTOPHER. Laugh?

ROBERT. When somebody hurts you, just laugh at them. You don't care. They'll soon get the message. *(Pause.)*

CHRISTOPHER. Laugh, yeah?

ROBERT. It drives them crazy. Really, it's a good trick.

CHRISTOPHER. Oh I get you. Laugh. Really. HA HA HA HA HA. HA HA HA HA HA. "Laugh and the whole world laughs with you." AND THEN THEY LOCK YOU UP! What the fuck are you on about, man? D'you know what I mean? Pull yourself together!

ROBERT. OK. Cry. Do handstands. Express Yourself. Just Don't Take It Personally.

CHRISTOPHER. "Express myself." And who are you: "Professor Groovy"?

ROBERT. Strictly speaking it's "Doctor Groovy." N'ha ha ha ha. N'ha ha ha. See? You can do it. *(Silence.)* No. You're quite right. I'm sorry. But you see the thing is, Chris, I don't think that you are ill and I want you to try to settle down somewhere.

CHRISTOPHER. What I'm saying is Doctor, I been unlucky where I been housed, yeah?

ROBERT. Well then … you need to be re-housed not locked up. *(Pause.)*

CHRISTOPHER. I think Bruce is right. I'm not ready. I don't wanna go.

ROBERT. OK … well … did he actually say that to you, did he?

CHRISTOPHER. He asked me if I was sure.

ROBERT. And you said you were, didn't you?

CHRISTOPHER. Yeah but I was lying. D'you know what I mean? *(Pause.)*

ROBERT. You were *lying*.

CHRISTOPHER. I was lying.

ROBERT. Why?

CHRISTOPHER. 'Cos I wanted to get out of this place.

ROBERT. A-ha! "The truth will out." You "wanted to get out of this place." You did. It's true.

CHRISTOPHER. But now I don't.

ROBERT. Yes you do.

CHRISTOPHER. No I don't.

ROBERT. I think you do.

CHRISTOPHER. I fucking don't, man.

ROBERT. You do and I'm going to continue to suggest to you that you do whether your conscious mind likes it or not. *(Pause.)* You see, until your *conscious* mind catches up with what your *subconscious* mind wants ... and *knows,* which is that you, quote, "want to get out of here" unquote, you're never going to get better. And you're never going to get out of here.

CHRISTOPHER. I'm never...?

ROBERT. Nope. Never. You'll be in hospital — this hospital or some other hospital somewhere — in and out of hospital for the rest of your life. For the rest of your life. *(Pause.)*

CHRISTOPHER. Now I'm scared.

ROBERT. Sure. Of course you are. And I think that's right. I think if you weren't nervous, you wouldn't be human.

CHRISTOPHER. I didn't say I was nervous.

ROBERT. Well ... I think you are.

CHRISTOPHER. Oh man. What am I gonna do?

ROBERT. I've just told you what to do.

CHRISTOPHER. Uh?

ROBERT. I just told you what you should do. *(Christopher stares into space.)* Chris...? The Council...? Your housing officer —

CHRISTOPHER. He said I could stay. Doctor Flaherty said —

ROBERT. You know what I think? I think that you *think* you are scared. And that's all it is, a thought. And I think that it's not your thought.

CHRISTOPHER. What d'you mean?

ROBERT. I think that someone else's thoughts have scared you.

CHRISTOPHER. You think ... I'm thinking someone else's thoughts? *(Pause.)* Whose thoughts?

ROBERT. I'm saying ... look ... Maybe Doctor Flaherty "projected" his fears of letting you go home onto you and now they're *your* fears. I'm saying maybe, just maybe Doctor Flaherty … unconsciously put his thoughts into your head.

CHRISTOPHER. He put his thoughts in my head. In *my* head…?

ROBERT. Look, this morning, you were ready to go home. You were so excited. You couldn't wait. You wanted coffee, you had your bags packed, wa — hey it was all happening for you. Remember?

CHRISTOPHER. Mm …

ROBERT. So what's changed? What's new my friend? Eh? *(Pause.)* *Nothing.* You had your bags packed. *(Pause.)* Nothing has changed. You're going home. Stop thinking about it. Just do it.

CHRISTOPHER. But, see the thing is, I got the impression, I got the impression from Doctor Flaherty —

ROBERT. What? Did he say something? What did he say?

CHRISTOPHER. No but I got the impression —

ROBERT. Well did you read his mind? *(Christopher stares. Silence.)* OK forget that, bad idea. But but but … what I'm saying is How Do You Know? Because really: he wants you to go too. He wants rid of you. I should know.

CHRISTOPHER. He wants rid of me?

ROBERT. Yes. He's had enough of you my friend, we all have. Don't jolly well … outstay your welcome! N'huh huh huh. Go. Be free. *(Pause.)* N'huh huh huh. D'you see? *(Pause.)* I'm trying to help you.

CHRISTOPHER. I read his mind?

ROBERT. I said to forget that.

CHRISTOPHER. He wants rid of me?

ROBERT. I'm joking. It's a joke!

CHRISTOPHER. The oranges are blue. *(Silence.)* Remember he asked me what colour the orange was?

ROBERT. Mm.

CHRISTOPHER. And I said it was blue. It was. I *saw* that. *(Pause.)* Bright blue. Virtually glowing.

ROBERT. You've had a psychotic episode. Things will be a bit strange for a while. Nothing more insidious.

CHRISTOPHER. "A bit strange"? They were blue.

ROBERT. We will give you medication for that.

46

CHRISTOPHER. I'm seeing things.

ROBERT. OK OK OK look. You're not.

CHRISTOPHER. What?

ROBERT. You're not seeing things. I think … all right … I think you wanted so badly to stay here, subconsciously, that you think you saw things, or you *said* you saw things …

CHRISTOPHER. You saying I was lying? *Me?*

ROBERT. N … I'm saying you were lying. Yes.

CHRISTOPHER. Well I think *you're* lying. *(Pause.)* You're prolly not even a proper doctor.

ROBERT. Well … n'ha … I can assure you Chris, I am a "proper doctor."

CHRISTOPHER. Prove it.

ROBERT. I don't have to prove it.

CHRISTOPHER. Well that's not fair is it? What about my job? D'you know what I mean? I got a job to go to. On a fruit stall. In the market. I *sell* oranges. *(Pause.)*

ROBERT. You sell oranges? (I didn't know that …)

CHRISTOPHER. It's true. What am I supposed to tell the customers? I'm in no condition to sell fruit, d'you know what I saying? Same as I say, I got problems. *(Pause.)*

ROBERT. Well. OK. In fact, as I remember, and correct me if I'm wrong: *First,* Doctor Flaherty *told* you it wasn't orange. The first thing he said was: "It's not an orange orange." What does that tell you? You spontaneously made what's called a "Common Association." You may just have easily said Red. It's harmless.

CHRISTOPHER. It means something.

ROBERT. What does it mean?

CHRISTOPHER. It's a sign. 'Cos nobody believes me but I think it proves it. He likes oranges. Every day a shipment from Nairobi. I just *proved* that. I come in here, first thing I see, oranges! They turn blue. A *signal. (Pause.)*

ROBERT. OK look … we don't have to concern ourselves with these things now.

CHRISTOPHER. Yeah but I'm worried now. I got the fear.

ROBERT. There's nothing to be afraid of.

CHRISTOPHER. You don't know that.

ROBERT. I do, yes, I do. Because. Two reasons. I'll tell you then you'll promise to stop fretting about them, OK? Two things. One: We can sort these things out when you get home. It's unfair for you to be here while we answer those questions. They are not life threatening. They are not a danger to you. You are not a danger to yourself. You'll be seeing me once a month and you'll be quite Safe and so now I want you to forget all about it.

CHRISTOPHER. Seeing *you?*

ROBERT. If I take over your case yes. That might happen.

CHRISTOPHER. Why should I see you?

ROBERT. Because it's what I think is best. Because ... it would be a "shame" if you didn't. *(Pause.)*

CHRISTOPHER. Yeah but I wanna see Doctor Flaherty.

ROBERT. I'd be better.

CHRISTOPHER. Uh huh. *(Pause.)* What's the other thing? You said there was two.

ROBERT. The *second* thing is ... *(Pause.)* Doctor Flaherty ... Bruce ... is somewhat *Unorthodox* in his approach. What he's suggesting by keeping you in here is, you have to understand, a little unorthodox. We don't do that anymore if we can help it. We want you out there. We want you to go *home.* D'you see?

CHRISTOPHER. Yeah but he's worried that's all.

ROBERT. I know and that's because, you see, Bruce, Bruce, see Bruce is a little, as we say in the trade, He's a Tee-Pee And A Wig-Wam. *(Pause.)* He's Too Tense. *(Pause.)* Heh heh. No I'm kidding. But he is ... you know, he's just a, you know, *I'm* the Head Of Department. I'm the Boss. I'm The Big Cheese. *(Pause.)* The Top Banana. *(Pause.)* OK this is very delicate. It's not something we know an awful lot about. But it's my specific field of research, I'm writing a Book on it as a matter of fact.

CHRISTOPHER. You're writing a book? Really? You're really writing a book?

ROBERT. Well ... I blush to the toes of my shoes to admit but ...

CHRISTOPHER. What's it about?

ROBERT. Well ... it's about ... it's about psychosis diagnosis. In ... people like you.

CHRISTOPHER. People like me, yeah?

ROBERT. You see, I believe there may be a Cognitive Therapy which we can substitute for the Drug Palliatives normally associated with psychosis. My "Assertion" is this: There is a Cultural Specificity to the apparently delusionary nature of some of your beliefs. There are Antecedents for some of the beliefs you hold. "Cultural Specificity and Cultural Antecedent Or Schizophrenia." You see? "*Or* Schizophrenia." Not "And." That's what it's called. *(Pause.)*

CHRISTOPHER. Sounds like a smash hit to me, man. What does Doctor Flaherty think about it?

ROBERT. Well … uh … he hasn't read it yet.

CHRISTOPHER. I meant about me seeing you.

ROBERT. Oh well … OK … well the thing is … see … *(Pause.)* Doctor Flaherty isn't in possession of the full facts.

CHRISTOPHER. Why not?

ROBERT. Because he's not an authority. I'm an authority. He isn't. *(Pause.)* Because there are things you do and things you believe which he, within his culture, can only recognize as Insanity. *(Pause.)*

CHRISTOPHER. Insanity.

ROBERT. It means he has a tendency to overlook, in our discussions at any rate, your cultural identity. *(Pause.)* It's nothing … it's no big deal … it's an oversight, that's all. It's a vastly complex subject. People get things wrong.

CHRISTOPHER. What did he say?

ROBERT. Well … well … since you asked … I think he has a very real fear that … our response to you is weighted by our response to your colour. I personally feel that *should* be the case; it *should* be a factor in your treatment and that we shouldn't overlook such a thing. Otherwise what happens, in institutions such as this, there develops what's termed "Ethnocentricity"; which ordinarily is fairly harmless but in certain instances is not far off … well … it is the progenitor of "Cultural Oppression," which in turn leads to what we call "Institutionalized Racism."

CHRISTOPHER. Racism?

ROBERT. Yes. And the danger is that in a sense you maybe end up, in a sense, being "punished" for the colour of your skin. *(Beat.)* For your ethnicity and your attendant cultural beliefs. *(Beat.)* You are Sectioned and locked up when you shouldn't be. *(Beat.)* Because you're "black." *(Pause.)*

CHRISTOPHER. I'm being *punished*?

ROBERT. Maybe that's too strong a term but but but —

CHRISTOPHER. Because I'm *black?*

ROBERT. Well you see, the system is *flawed.* People of ethnic minority are not well catered for, it's a well-known fact. I've just expressed it clumsily —

CHRISTOPHER. He said that? I'm locked up because I'm black? *(Christopher stands up abruptly.)*

ROBERT. No that's not what was said. Let me finish ...

CHRISTOPHER. Where is he?

ROBERT. OK calm down.

CHRISTOPHER. The fuck does that mean?

ROBERT. Chris Chris Chris Chris —

CHRISTOPHER. He really said that? It's 'cos I'm black? *(Christopher heads for the door, and Robert rushes around and blocks his way, trying to hold him back.)*

ROBERT. *(Struggling with him.)* Look, listen, look, listen, look, listen, look, listen, look, listen ... *(Pause.)* Chris, my dear dear fellow, just sit down and listen for one moment please. Our Colonial Antecedents are latent and barely suppressed —

CHRISTOPHER. What shit! *(He paces angrily.)*

ROBERT. This is really a storm in a tea cup.

CHRISTOPHER. Punished by who?

ROBERT. Chris please, sit down. Sit down. Come on now. I implore you. *(Christopher sits and thinks, stares, quiet.)*

CHRISTOPHER. Who am I being punished by?

ROBERT. Well, by, by, by, the *system.* The system tends to punish without meaning to.

CHRISTOPHER. That's why I see things? I'm being punished?

ROBERT. No ... Chris —

CHRISTOPHER. That's why I hear things? These *mental* ... *fucking* ... the noises I hear ... the *fear* —

ROBERT. What he said was —

CHRISTOPHER. You said I'm not thinking my own thoughts —

ROBERT. No —

CHRISTOPHER. Well whose thoughts am I thinking?

ROBERT. Nobody —

CHRISTOPHER. Doctor Flaherty's...?

ROBERT. OK let's not get off the track —

CHRISTOPHER. He smokes too much *drugs,* man, d'you know

what I mean? He likes his puff. I can tell. *(Silence.)*

ROBERT. Sorry ... you said? About ... dr...?

CHRISTOPHER. He *told* me I should go back out there and *score* some puff, man. Why did he say that? Because I'm black?

ROBERT. O ... K ... but ... I'm sure ... *(Pause.)* "Puff." For him...? Or ... for...?

CHRISTOPHER. He goes he goes he goes, If I was only in here to get drugs I'd come to the wrong place. He said the drugs out there, right, were more *fun.*

ROBERT. I see, well ... I see ... well. *(Beat.)* When was this?

CHRISTOPHER. Earlier. Before you got here.

ROBERT. Just before or ... some time before —

CHRISTOPHER. Just before. This morning.

ROBERT. Oh. *(Pause.)* What else did he say?

CHRISTOPHER. He said it was "Voodoo." That's why I'm here. Voodoo. Remember?

ROBERT. W ... ell ...

CHRISTOPHER. And he lied to me. He said he was letting me out when he was just gonna keep me in here longer just like you said, man. He lied to me. *(Pause.)* And and he keeps looking at me funny. *(Pause.)* Can I have a cup of coffee now? *(Blackout.)*

ACT THREE

Next afternoon. Bruce and Christopher sit facing each other;
the bowl of oranges is on the table between them. Bruce has
a report in front of him and is reading from it. Christopher
is smoking a cigarette and staring into space.

BRUCE. "He ordered the patient to peel the orange … " I didn't
order you. *(He reads.)* " … Establishing that it was the same under
the skin. That the flesh was the same colour as the skin." OK I *sug-*
gested, Chris, I *prompted,* and maybe I shouldn't have but, you
know, it's not as if this was the first time was it? You don't need my
help to start … *(Reading.)* seeing things … *(He reads.)* "He
snatched away a cup of coffee given to the patient by the
Consultant … He used the pejorative epithet 'nigger.'" *(Silence.)* I
did not, um, my God, I didn't use the epithet … nnn … *(He*
stares.) I did not call you a … um, um, um, a … I didn't say that.
CHRISTOPHER. Say what?
BRUCE. Would you please put that out? Christopher? The cigarette. *(Christopher mashes out the cigarette on the table.)* I, I, I, didn't
call you a, a, a, um, a … a … *(Beat.)* "Nigger."
CHRISTOPHER. You said "uppity nigga." You did. Deny.
BRUCE. Only because *you* did. My God! It was a quote!
CHRISTOPHER. Yeah but you shouldn'ta said it.
BRUCE. Oh so so so only you can say it?
CHRISTOPHER. It's not polite.
BRUCE. I know it isn't and, um … I'm sorry, excuse me … I feel
sick … *(He steadies himself. Pause.)* Do, do you really think I meant
it? Do you really think I meant to "provoke" you? I was giving vent
to "racist" proclivities?
CHRISTOPHER. Look. I don't know. I don't know. I just want
to go home.
BRUCE. What is wrong with you? Are you out of your mind?

Have you been drinking? *(Robert appears in the doorway, listening. He enters and sits down.)*

ROBERT. You asked to see me.

BRUCE. We have a meeting. *(Pause.)* We agreed to meet today. The three of us. Unless you know of something that could have happened to change that.

ROBERT. I'm on the Authority Doctor Flaherty, of course I know. *(Pause.)* There was a Management Hearing this morning.

BRUCE. Yes I know. How convenient. *(Robert shrugs.)* So. Where do we go from here?

ROBERT. Well, you know, actually, what I think is that you and I need to be alone together.

BRUCE. OK. Uh. Christopher would you mind coming back in … *(He checks his watch.)*

CHRISTOPHER. But I've just packed.

BRUCE. That's all right. Just go back to your ward and I'll send for you.

CHRISTOPHER. But I've just —

BRUCE. Please Chris.

CHRISTOPHER. But we —

BRUCE. Please?

CHRISTOPHER. But … I'm getting out today. My twenty-eight —

BRUCE. OK look —

CHRISTOPHER. My twenty-eight —

BRUCE. Chris —

CHRISTOPHER. My twenty —

BRUCE. I know but —

CHRISTOPHER. My —

BRUCE. All right! *(Pause.)* Not now. *Later.* I'll send for you.

CHRISTOPHER. I already packed.

BRUCE. I know. *(Christopher stands and exits.)*

ROBERT. I know exactly what you're thinking and before you say anything I want you to know it was nothing to do with me. *(Beat.)* I mean, whatever he said to the *rest* of the Authority … *(Beat.)* I had no idea that he'd done this when I went into that Management Hearing this morning. I knew he wanted to make a complaint to the Authority — I tried to talk him out of it. That's

53

the last I knew of it.

BRUCE.   But you "are the Authority."

ROBERT.   OK ... I'm a *Representative at Management Hearings.*
One of many.

BRUCE.   But yesterday you said you "are the Authority."

ROBERT.   Only sometimes ... sometimes it's me, yes, who ...
whoever is ... *everybody* runs it. It's a different person each week
depending on ... it's more of a *committee* than a, than a ...

BRUCE.   The point is ... have you read this? *(Pause.)*

ROBERT.   Of course I've read it.

BRUCE.   Don't tell me. You've read it because: you wrote it?

ROBERT.   Of course I didn't write it. What kind of bastard do
you take me for? *(Pause.)*

BRUCE.   *(Reading.)* "After some initial difficulty following the
patient's interpretation of events, the Authority reached a consensus that if the said orange was indeed to be viewed as blue for the
purpose of the analogy ... " For the purposes of...? *(He gives Robert
a look.)* " ... then clearly as a blue-skinned orange it was indeed in
the minority given that other citruses are ordinarily orange, yellow
or ... in the case of limes, lime green." *(He gives Robert a look.)* "By
asking the patient to peel the 'minority' orange ... and declaring
the insides of the orange to be of equally unusual colouring, the
Registrar seems to have implied ... " What did you *say* to him?

ROBERT.   I didn't say anything. *(Bruce reads.)*

BRUCE.   "The Authority reached a consensus." How? Did everybody think of the the the stupidest things they could think of and
then put them all in a hat? By playing a drinking game? Small
children wouldn't come up with this. *Monkeys* could do better
using *sign language.* For God's sake!

ROBERT.   "Monkeys."

BRUCE.   Yes.

ROBERT.   Is that another analogy? *(Bruce stares.)* It's too easy to
misinterpret Bruce. You really have to be more careful.

BRUCE.   Well. Do you agree with "The Authority"?

ROBERT.   I rather think I should remain impartial on this one.
Besides, they're more interested in your side of the story. Give me
a Statement and they'll probably leave you alone.

BRUCE.   Give you a "Statement." But I haven't done anything! I can't ... believe ... has it really gone that far? Can't you ... can't I just talk to them?

ROBERT. Well ... not really. There's a Procedure. *(Pause. Bruce reads.)*

BRUCE. "The Authority recommends that a senior Consultant confers treatment with an outpatient programme."

ROBERT. I think it's a good idea.

BRUCE. Why?

ROBERT. I'm a Senior Consultant. He already knows me.

BRUCE. What do you get out of it?

ROBERT. I don't "get" anything. It's just Expediency.

BRUCE. "Expediency." The Path Of Least Resistance.

ROBERT. Absolutely.

BRUCE. OK. So. You want me to take over the case. And ... *(Pause.)* Then you can continue Your Research? *(Pause.)* And Then You Can Finish Your Book. Is it a good book? It must be, you'll go to any lengths to finish it ...

ROBERT. You're on very thin ice here Flaherty.

BRUCE. "The Search for the Holy Grail." What a chapter heading that would make. "A Cure For Black Psychosis." Imagine. No more bed Crises. No more hospitals. We'd save a bundle on Care In The Community. You'd become Professor overnight.

ROBERT. I *beg* your pardon!

BRUCE. You heard.

ROBERT. Are you out of your mind?

BRUCE. You'll be the toast of Academia the World Over. Imagine! A golden opportunity to distinguish yourself from all the other boffins; to be the Eggiest Egg Head of them all. To be *different* from all the other odious little careerists on the gravy train kissing management arse. To be Up There with all the other Cambridge wonderboys in their bow ties and tweed, flapping about the "corridors of power" with their pricks in each other's pockets. What's wrong with just *doing your job? (Pause.)*

ROBERT. It's the Maudsley actually.

BRUCE. I'm sorry?

ROBERT. I read Psychiatry at the Institute of Psychiatry at the Maudsley Hospital in Camberwell. Not Cambridge.

BRUCE. Oh, the Maudsley, big difference.

ROBERT. I really recommend you go there. I think you need to go there. And I don't mean for training. *(Pause.)* You're already the subject of an inquiry. If the Authority asks for a Psychiatric Report I'll be in a very awkward position. *(Silence.)*

BRUCE. OK. OK. Look … have you never heard … listen, uh, Doctor … did you hear Christopher refer to himself, somewhat effacingly, somewhat ironically, as a, quote, "uppity nigger"? Did you hear him say that?

ROBERT. It was unmistakable.

BRUCE. And presumably you heard me quoting him, also, I offer, somewhat ironically?

ROBERT. I'd steer clear of irony if I were you. You're not Lenny Bruce.

BRUCE. It was … it was a *nuance*. It was … the way I said it … with a note of familiarity … because I know him … and —

ROBERT. It's not for me to characterize your "nuances," — Doctor. And if you ask me, yes, perhaps it was somewhat "provocative and unorthodox."

BRUCE. Only to you.

ROBERT. How do you mean?

BRUCE. It was provocative and unorthodox to you because, well, frankly, it would be wouldn't it? Perhaps you don't get out enough.

ROBERT. You're doing it again: you're being provocative. *(Pause.)* You know what I mean. *(Bruce seizes the report and tears it into bits. Robert produces a mobile phone and dials.)* This is Doctor Robert Smith, can somebody send Christopher over here immediately please … upstairs … yes … no, I'm in the consultation room with Doctor Flaherty … no he's my … no he was but … he … n … I understand but … well he's my patient now. *(He puts the phone away.)*

BRUCE. What did you tell him?

ROBERT. Bruce —

BRUCE. What have you done?

ROBERT. It's his complaint; why don't you just ask him?

BRUCE. I intend to. (Just as soon as you've slithered off.)

ROBERT. Actually, that's not possible I'm afraid. Not until I've briefed the patient.

BRUCE. … What?

ROBERT. That's the procedure. I can't allow you to be alone with him. It's a question of Seniority as much as anything else. Perhaps if you'd shown some respect for Seniority in the first place; if you'd listened to Somebody Who Knew, we wouldn't be in this mess.

BRUCE. So I'm not allowed to see Chris any more without you present?

ROBERT. Anything you want to ask you must ask the Authority.

BRUCE. I just *asked* "The Authority" and I think "The Authority"'s *lying.*

ROBERT. I'm presenting you with the opportunity to defend yourself. That's the Procedure. What more do you want?

BRUCE. Christ, it's so transparent.

ROBERT. Oh do stop whining, Bruce. Before somebody nails you to a cross. *(Pause.)* Oh. While I'm here I should mention that I've been keeping a diary.

BRUCE. A *diary?*

ROBERT. A diary of my research but there are things in it which might be relevant to your case. *(He produces a diary from his jacket pocket.)* Now you've stopped blustering I should read you some things before my patient returns.

BRUCE. You just happened to have it on you.

ROBERT. *(Reading.)* "Twenty-sixth of October: Mention Antecedent Programme to Doctor Flaherty and he laughs. Not interested in providing African-Caribbean and African patients for research purposes."

BRUCE. I didn't laugh ... I ... this is silly ...

ROBERT. Which suggests you have been obstructive towards me from the off. I'm your *Supervisor.* You don't turn down a request like that unless you have a very good reason.

BRUCE. I ... look ... I have professional reservations ... ethical reservations about —

ROBERT. About what?

BRUCE. About using patients as, as guinea pigs in, in, in —

ROBERT. "Guinea pigs"? Honestly Bruce "Monkeys, guinea pigs, voodoo ... " You've an entire menagerie of piccaninny slurs to unleash.

BRUCE. *What?*

ROBERT. Can you not see how this could be *interpreted* — by the Authority for example? You have to admit it doesn't look good.

BRUCE. Then don't show it to the Authority.

ROBERT. I beg your pardon.

BRUCE. I said don't ... show ... Doctor Smith ... please ... it's ... it's ... do we have to show them this?

ROBERT. We'll pretend you didn't say that, shall we? *(Silence. Bruce just stares. Robert flips over a few pages.)*

ROBERT. "Twenty-fourth of October: Flaherty implies research funds being used to keep me in, quote, 'dickie bows and putters.'"

BRUCE. We were *drunk*. After the rugby.

ROBERT. *You* were drunk.

BRUCE. And and and you *agreed* with me. It was a joke!

ROBERT. You invite me to watch the rugby with you and then you insult me. You drag me home for a chunk of rancid cheese on toast, get pissy-drunk on Bulgarian Hock and start haranguing me about iniquity in the Medical Profession like some kind of mildly retarded Student Activist, then you expect the Nobel Peace Prize For Services To Psychiatry. Why are you so threatened by my ideas?

BRUCE. Because ... *(Pause.)* Because they're *shit* doctor. The research is banal and it's all been done before *anyway*. It's Old News. It's R.D. *Laing* in a gorilla suit. It isn't Empirical. And it isn't a Ph.D. It isn't a Book. A *cook book* would be more ground-breaking. It's a waste of resources and money and everybody's time and you know it.

ROBERT. What are you implying? *(Pause.)* You see, this is just the type of verbiage —

BRUCE. Verbiage?

ROBERT. Which people find so highly offensive about you Bruce. This is how you wind up under investigation. *(Christopher walks in carrying a large hold-all and sits down.)*

CHRISTOPHER. Hope I'm not interrupting.

ROBERT. Hello again Christopher. I'm so sorry to send you away like that. We've concluded our meeting now and as soon as the doctor has asked you one or two more questions you'll be on your way.

CHRISTOPHER. I'm going home now?

ROBERT. You're going home.

CHRISTOPHER. Oh boy. Oh man. I'm going home.

BRUCE. Chris, have I upset you in any way?

ROBERT. You can't ask that question.

BRUCE. Why — because he might answer it?

ROBERT. Jurisprudence dictates.

BRUCE. Are there "charges pending"?

ROBERT. You are Under Investigation, yes. If there are charges to be answered then you will be suspended pending the Inquiry.

BRUCE. What charges.

ROBERT. Negligence.

BRUCE. "Negligence"?

ROBERT. Racial Harassment.

BRUCE. What else? I'm intrigued.

ROBERT. Abuse.

BRUCE. "Abuse." Well. I was waiting for that. "Abuse." Mm. You know what I think? I think people abuse the term "Abuse."

ROBERT. Excuse us for a moment please Christopher. *(Robert takes Bruce by the elbow and marches him into the far corner of the room.)* Doctor Flaherty, if Christopher stays in here indefinitely under a Section 3 and is diagnosed with Paranoid Schizophrenia, the rest of his life will be ruined.

BRUCE. He won't get the help he needs without that diagnosis.

ROBERT. It would be negligent.

BRUCE. Please, Doctor Smith, yours is an *arbitrary diagnosis.* You've observed him in more than one interview. It's my word against yours.

ROBERT. Two interviews.

BRUCE. And you saw something entirely different to what I've seen.

ROBERT. That's the ICD 10 for you. Observation and interview.

BRUCE. I think … look I think he's suicidal.

ROBERT. He's not suicidal. He's just depressed.

BRUCE. He's depressed because he's Schizophrenic.

ROBERT. He's depressed because he's *here.* Exactly how old is Christopher?

BRUCE. He's the same age as me.

ROBERT. The same age as you. And how do you think it feels for Christopher — a bright, fun, charismatic young man — to be locked up with chronic, dysfunctional mental patients twice his age? People with drug problems, who are suicidally depressed, who scream and laugh and cry routinely for no apparent reason — when they're not *catatonic*. Have you thought about how intimidating and frightening that must be for him? Night after night after night, with no let up. It's Like Going To Prison. It's *cruel*. *(Silence.)* Now. I have examined the patient in depth. I have consulted with a social worker and a CPN.

BRUCE. When?

ROBERT. In this morning's Management Hearing. And we believe this patient will receive the treatment he needs in the Community. We believe that we would be failing him by keeping him.

BRUCE. So ... it's all been settled then. I'm being over-ruled.

ROBERT. To say the fucking least, Doctor.

BRUCE. So why have an Inquiry.

ROBERT. Well, you see, for what it's worth, we're beginning to wonder whether this patient should ever have been Sectioned in the first place.

BRUCE. The, the, the police Sectioned him with a 136.

ROBERT. Well perhaps they were being "Ethnocentric." He was drinking. He was depressed. The hospitals are full of men like Christopher. The prisons are full of men like Christopher. Ordinary men whose lives have flown apart and they've found themselves in a market one day "acting funny." Next day they've been locked up and a week later they're on the coast of a crack-up. Don't you think it's time we did something about it? *(Pause.)* Look at him! He's a *mess*. Well? What have you got to say for yourself? *(Pause. To Christopher.)* I'm sorry Chris.

CHRISTOPHER. No, you just talk amongst yourselves. D'you know what I mean? *(Bruce stares into space. Silence.)*

BRUCE. You're not going to show me any support here are you? As my Supervisor? As a Mentor? A friend?

ROBERT. That would be highly inappropriate.

BRUCE. You've made up your mind. You support this allegation.

ROBERT. Not the allegation, just the Inquiry. I'm afraid so.

BRUCE. Gee Whiz. Just wait till I tell my wife. *(Pause.)* Maybe *you'd* like to tell her. Next time we invite you for dinner. Next time she slaves over a hot stove to put food in your mouth.

ROBERT. I'd hardly call Welsh Rarebit "slavery."

BRUCE. Next time I buy you a ticket for the rugby.

ROBERT. If you'd let me buy them we'd have sat in the Member's stand.

BRUCE. I don't even *like* fucking rugby. Bunch of hairy *twats* running around biting each others' ears off. *(Pause.)*

ROBERT. Bruce, I'm simply asking you to give me a Statement. Give the Authority your side of the story. Now. Have you got a lawyer?

BRUCE. Why should *I* get a lawyer? *You* get a lawyer. *Prove* this. I can't believe this is even happening!

ROBERT. I really don't understand why you're taking it so personally. Why are you so angry?

BRUCE. Because it *is* personal. You're somebody I trusted. I confided in. I thought you were on my side. I thought you and me could make a difference. Which is why I invited you over. My wife cooked. Nourished you. I should have choked you.

ROBERT. Bruce. You wanted me for your Supervisor. Your Mentor. You expect me to recommend your Consultancy one day.

BRUCE. And why did you agree — if not to get research material out of me? To finish your book. To ... to ... Doctor Sm ... please ... I don't know why ...

ROBERT. I agreed because I liked you. I thought you had a promise. I thought, such is my vanity, that you could learn something from me. Is that so difficult to believe? Are you really so insecure? *(Silence. They stare at each other.)*

CHRISTOPHER. You got any Jelly Babies?

BRUCE. *(To Christopher.)* Did I upset you yesterday? When I asked you to peel that orange? *(Bruce tosses Christopher an orange from the bowl and he catches it.)*

ROBERT. I really don't think this is a good idea.

BRUCE. Did that upset you? *(Christopher looks at Robert.)* No don't look at him, look at me.

CHRISTOPHER. D'you know what I mean? I'm thirsty. I need a Coke.

BRUCE. You'll get a Coke if you answer my question.

ROBERT. Doctor Flaherty.

BRUCE. Did that upset you when you peeled the orange.

CHRISTOPHER. No.

BRUCE. Later, when you got to thinking about it, were you upset?

CHRISTOPHER. No. It interested me.

ROBERT. You're pushing your luck, Flaherty.

BRUCE. "No"? Oh, OK. Why do you think I asked you to peel the orange?

CHRISTOPHER. To see what colour it was inside.

BRUCE. And what colour was it? In your own words. Without any help from me.

CHRISTOPHER. In my own words. Blue.

BRUCE. Peel another one. See if it's still blue.

ROBERT. I really don't recommend this.

BRUCE. Go ahead Christopher. Why not? I'll even let you eat it. *(Pause. Christopher peels the orange. Pause. He begins eating it suspiciously.)* What colour is the orange, Chris?

CHRISTOPHER. Blue.

BRUCE. OK. And what do you think that means? *(Pause.)*

CHRISTOPHER. Something to do with my dad.

ROBERT. OK that's enough.

BRUCE. Something to do with your dad? OK.

ROBERT. I said —

BRUCE. And what do you think I think it means?

ROBERT. Enough!

BRUCE. What do *I* think it *represents?*

CHRISTOPHER. S … omething to do with my dad?

ROBERT. This is not the time or the —

BRUCE. Any idea what?

ROBERT. … Place.

CHRISTOPHER. Nope. No idea, man.

BRUCE. Well, I have no idea either.

CHRISTOPHER. Maybe it's a signal.

ROBERT. I must insist —

BRUCE. Or a coincidence?

CHRISTOPHER. No it ain't a coincidence.

BRUCE. What is it a signal of then? *(Christopher produces the crumpled newspaper cutting from his pocket and smooths it out, shows it to Bruce who shakes his head slowly.)*

CHRISTOPHER. Idi Amin Dada. See? "*Da-da.*" That's another signal.

BRUCE. No Chris … I'm sorry … please. *(He touches Christopher on the arm.)* Put it away now. Concentrate.

ROBERT. Don't you think you're being a bit arbitrary.

BRUCE. What?

ROBERT. Why should he put it away?

BRUCE. "Why"?

ROBERT. Yes. He's not a child. Why should he? *(Pause.)*

BRUCE. Because he cut it out of a newspaper.

ROBERT. "Because he cu — " Really? *(Pause.)* And and and what makes you think that? *(Robert snatches the article from Christopher and examines it.)*

BRUCE. It's just a hunch.

ROBERT. Well, my hunch is that he didn't. My hunch is that his mother gave it to him. What is it about this particular disclosure that makes you so uncomfortable, Bruce?

BRUCE. What makes me uncomfortable is that this morning he told me his father was Muhammad Ali. He'd seen him on breakfast television winning Sports Personality of the Century. *(Silence.)*

ROBERT. *(To Christopher.)* Is this true?

CHRISTOPHER. 1974. *Zaire. Think* about it, man.

ROBERT. *(To Bruce.)* Why didn't you tell me this before?

BRUCE. Before when?

ROBERT. Before … *now. (Pause.)* You told me about his mother in Feltham, blue oranges and the Chevrolet but the rumble in the Bloody Fucking Jungle you didn't deem appropriate! Jesus wept! *(Silence.)* OK. Now. OK, what have we got here? One of the most feared men in history and one of the most loved. Both immensely powerful. Both role models. Both of African origins.

CHRISTOPHER. Both Muslim Fundamentalists.

ROBERT. Abso-fucking-lutely!

BRUCE. Christopher, please. I want you to concentrate on the orange —

ROBERT. I am warning you, Doctor —

BRUCE. What does it represent now?

ROBERT. It was stipulated at the Management Hearing that you have no further contact —

BRUCE. What do you think Doctor Smith thinks it represents.

ROBERT. Listen … Christopher —

CHRISTOPHER. That's easy —

ROBERT. Chris…? Bruce —
BRUCE. Robert — Chris —
ROBERT. Bruce — Chris —
BRUCE. *(To Robert.)* Grant me this one favour, please; listen to your patient. Chris?
CHRISTOPHER. He says it's a *Person.*
ROBERT. I never —
BRUCE. A person. What kind of person?
ROBERT. Said anything of the —
CHRISTOPHER. A Brother.
ROBERT. No. That's enough.
BRUCE. And do you agree with that?
CHRISTOPHER. I don't know.
ROBERT. What I said was … what I *meant* was … and you obviously completely misunderstood me … was —
CHRISTOPHER. You did —
ROBERT. Enough! Let me finish —
CHRISTOPHER. You said it was *Me.*
ROBERT. OK, OK, OK, OK, OK, OK, OK … OK … Now … I commented, I merely *reflected* that … . I *suggested* that it was an unfortunate demonstration which could potentially be viewed … by *somebody* very vulnerable … by a patient … as an "analogy."
BRUCE. But it wasn't an analogy.
ROBERT. All right … nevertheless … it could be "taken the wrong way." It could "cause offence" …
BRUCE. But it didn't cause offence —
ROBERT. Well … . in hindsight —
BRUCE. In whose hindsight?
ROBERT. OK all right, whatever the *fucking semantics,* it was an unfortunate incident —
BRUCE. It wasn't an accident —
ROBERT. All right, it was very, very … it was *upsetting.* He was upset by it, that's all and so, so, so I brought it up in the Management Hearing —
BRUCE. Oh *you* brought it up at the Management Hearing —
ROBERT. What?
BRUCE. You said you brought it up. You just said that. You said you brought it up at the Management Hearing this morning.

(Silence.)

CHRISTOPHER. And he said I should learn to lick my own balls. He did. Ridiculous but true. *(They all stare at each other. Robert rubs his eyes.)* (Do I look like a contortionist?)

BRUCE. So ... Doctor ... *you* made the Complaint. *You* lodged this Complaint with the Authority.

ROBERT. The patient was very upset. He was in no state to —

BRUCE. Were you upset Christopher?

CHRISTOPHER. What? When?

ROBERT. He was. Take my word for it.

BRUCE. *(To Christopher.)* Are you upset now?

ROBERT. I'm going to go berserk in a minute. I am trying to straighten this out for you! I am trying to *help*. *(Robert takes out his packet of cigarettes shakily. Lighting up.)* Give you the benefit of my ... erudition ... and experience ... as a Senior ... as Senior ... Senior Consultant ... *Head* of Department. *(Christopher takes a cigarette and the lighter and lights it, also shakily.)*

BRUCE. Christopher, if I upset you, I apologise. Sincerely. I didn't mean to upset you. Did I say anything else that upset you? *(Pause.)* Chris?

CHRISTOPHER. You put your thoughts in my head.

BRUCE. What kind of thoughts?

CHRISTOPHER. Just thoughts.

ROBERT. I have to insist this stops right now.

BRUCE. Shut up. Chris...?

ROBERT. Christopher. Not another word.

BRUCE. Can you think of anything specific? *(Christopher stares at Bruce. Christopher spits the orange out and stares at the remaining segments in his hand.)*

CHRISTOPHER. The thoughts I have are not my thoughts. He said that I think your thoughts.

BRUCE. Doctor *Smith* said?

CHRISTOPHER. And that's why I have to get out of here.

ROBERT. That's not what I said.

CHRISTOPHER. I've gotta get outta here 'cos of you, man!

ROBERT. Look ...

CHRISTOPHER. 'Cos you're *bad.*

ROBERT. OK ... Christopher —

CHRISTOPHER. And now I don't, I don't, I don't know what to think! I don't know what to think any more. When I do think, it's not my thoughts, it's not my voice when I talk. You tell me who I am. Who I'm not. I don't know who I am any more! I don't know who I am!

ROBERT. Chris —

BRUCE. Chris —

ROBERT. It's being here that's doing this to you. This place —

BRUCE. You're still very confused —

ROBERT. You can't think straight in this place. How can you…?

BRUCE. You're safe here, OK? It's quiet —

ROBERT. Apart from the bloodcurdling screams of all the other mental patients …

BRUCE. Chris you need to do this, you must try and stay a little longer —

ROBERT. You can leave now if you want to leave now —

BRUCE. Chris —

ROBERT. But you have to want to.

Christopher. I do want to!

BRUCE. Are you sure you're ready?

CHRISTOPHER. No man I'm not sure of anything!

ROBERT. Christopher —

BRUCE. Chris —

ROBERT. Listen … list —

BRUCE. Chris —

ROBERT. Chris — Bruce

BRUCE. Chris — Robert

ROBERT. Bruce — Christopher

BRUCE. Christopher

ROBERT. Christopher

CHRISTOPHER. OK OK OK JUST SHUT UP JUST SHUT THE FUCK UP FOR ONE MOMENT FOR GOD'S SAKE YOU ARE DRIVING ME AROUND THE BEND! *(Silence.)*

BRUCE. OK look … *(To Robert.)* Could we have a minute alone please?

ROBERT. Absolutely not.

BRUCE. I don't think you're in a position to argue any more.

ROBERT. You're only making it worse.

BRUCE. Nevertheless. I think you should.

ROBERT. OK! OK! It's *your funeral. (Robert exits. Silence.)*

CHRISTOPHER. What the fuck do you want, Bruce?

BRUCE. Well, um, well, um, I'd like you to understand that this is a very serious situation.

CHRISTOPHER. Yeah but the thing is, like he said, I don't think you should take it so personally, d'you know what I mean? *(Pause.)*

BRUCE. Well. You know. Um. I know. Yes. I'm trying.

CHRISTOPHER. When somebody does something you don't like, you should just learn to laugh. D'you understand?

BRUCE. Y — OK — OK. The thing is Chris ... see ... I'm not very good at this. I'm not very good at ... Not Taking Things Personally. That's all. I like to ... Get To The Bottom Of Things.

CHRISTOPHER. You don't say.

BRUCE. No I'm not being funny. Things here at the hospital, at work, I take personally sometimes. I'm ever mindful of the way one's *professional* life impacts upon one *personally*. Just as what happens to you here impacts upon *your* personal, private life. It's all related. So you see, when you took your complaint to the Authority one of things they concluded was that I had been "unprofessional." Which is in their jurisdiction to decide — they are generally more venerable — more experienced, judicious beings than I. However, the upshot is that depending on what happens now ... I could possibly be sacked in the *first month* of my Training! It isn't your fault. And I am not taking that personally. But what I would like to point out to you is that, that could well effect *both* or personal, private lives in a, in a *terrible, disastrous* way. OK? Do you understand now?

CHRISTOPHER. Don't patronize me. *(He eyeballs Bruce. Pause.)* I had a life before this. I had a job. On a stall in the market.

BRUCE. That's what I'm saying.

CHRISTOPHER. I got stuff to go back to. I've got my mum.

BRUCE. Your mum can't help you just now.

CHRISTOPHER. She needs me. She gets lonely. I miss her. *(Pause.)*

BRUCE. *(Gently.)* Chris ... you don't know where she is, do you? *(Pause.)* You see, my point is, when they let you out this afternoon, the theory is that you'll go back to your family. To your community. But you don't have a family do you? Not any more. Not so far as we know. And, the thing is, should you come back, should you ever need to return and ask for my help, I might not be here.

CHRISTOPHER. I'll see Doctor Smith.

BRUCE. I … I know. But, um … you can see him *anyway.*

CHRISTOPHER. How d'you mean?

BRUCE. There's no need for you to press ahead with this complaint. If you no longer want me to treat you, I won't.

CHRISTOPHER. I don't.

BRUCE. Then I won't. Fine.

CHRISTOPHER. 'Cos you put your thoughts in my head.

BRUCE. OK well … you know Chris, I really didn't mean to. Maybe other people have put thoughts in your head too but they're not going to be birched for it. Do you, do you, do you see what I mean?

CHRISTOPHER. No.

BRUCE. I'm saying … look … I don't know what Doctor Smith said to you yesterday evening, OK, I have no idea — actually, I have a pretty good idea and I think … I'll be honest with you. I think Doctor Smith "coached" you in what you had to say to the Authority. *(Pause.)* I think he put words in your mouth.

CHRISTOPHER. He put words in my *mouth?*

BRUCE. Yes. Not literally. Figuratively OK … don't get excited.

CHRISTOPHER. No, *You* put words in my mouth. When I said I wanted to stay and I was scared, that was you. That's why I'm here now! 'Cos of *you!*

BRUCE. No. OK? Now … no. Just … No. Just let me read you something. *(He takes a pamphlet from Christopher's file.)* I'm going to give you this to take with you. Whether you stay or go. This is what the World Health Organization has to say about Schizophrenia. I don't want to alarm you, but I want to explain to you what you've just said. I want to "demystify." *(He reads.)* "The most intimate thoughts … are often felt to be known or shared by others and explanatory delusions may develop, to the effect that natural or supernatural forces are at work to influence the individual's thoughts and actions in ways that are often bizarre." Sound familiar? *(Long pause. Christopher snatches the pamphlet, screws it up, throws it on the floor.)*

CHRISTOPHER. You're just trying to get off the hook now.

BRUCE. Just listen to me. You don't know what you're talking about.

CHRISTOPHER. Why? 'Cos I'm an "uppity nigga"?

BRUCE. Look. Shut up a minute.

CHRISTOPHER. Oh, that's very nice, that's lovely. It's all coming out now. *(Bruce slams his fist on the table.)*

BRUCE. This isn't a game! My career is on the line!

CHRISTOPHER. Your "career"?

BRUCE. And your .... your ... you have got so much to *lose!* We both have, don't you see this? *(Christopher kisses his teeth.)* Chris ... please for God's sake. Can you remember what you did in the market with the orange? Can you see how that could get you into a lot of trouble? If you were doing that ... on the estate, for example, I don't know what could happen ...

CHRISTOPHER. I never trusted you. Mm-mm. I liked you, but I never trusted you.

BRUCE. What...?

CHRISTOPHER. You told me I could have a Coke, yeah? In front of a witness you said I could have a Coke if I answered your questions and I answered your questions so where is it? D'you think I'm thick or something? D'you think I'm thick? You told me you were letting me out and now you're not. What's going on, Bruce?

BRUCE. I am, Christopher. I will.

CHRISTOPHER. When?

BRUCE. Soon.

CHRISTOPHER. Oh "soon."

BRUCE. When you've been diagnosed properly. You must try and be patient.

CHRISTOPHER. I don't *believe* you. You call me a nigga. You say it's voodoo.

BRUCE. It was a joke!

CHRISTOPHER. Oh funny joke. Do you see me laughing? I've got one for you. I'm gonna press Charges. 'Cos I ain't staying here, man. You'll never keep me locked up, white man. This is one nigga you don't Get to keep, white man. 'Cos I'm gonna bark every time you come near. D'you understand?

BRUCE. Is this You or is it ... someone else? Is this the *illness* or is it ... *(Pause.)* Maybe you're just *like* this. Maybe you're just ... A Wanker. I mean ... why do you say these things?

CHRISTOPHER. 'Cos you ruined my life! 'Cos you're Evil. And you're a Fascist.

BRUCE. How dare you! *(Bruce stands. Christopher stands.)* You fucking idiot ... What Have You *Done? (Christopher starts to laugh.)* What's funny? Stop laughing! Shut up! You stupid fucker. What are you laughing at? *(Robert is standing in the doorway, unseen.)* Shut up! For fuck's sake!

CHRISTOPHER. The look on your face boy!

BRUCE. You won't be laughing when you get home. You won't be laughing when you start losing your marbles all over again and hearing voices and jabbering like a lunatic and shitting yourself because you think your fucking zombie neighbors are coming to eat your brains you mad bastard! You *idiot!*

CHRISTOPHER. "Love Thy Neighbor" it says. How can I love my neighbour when my neighbour is Fascist?

BRUCE. They're black! All your neighbours are. It's a *Black Neighbourhood.* You you you *moron.* You stupid *fool.* Are you *retarded?* Jesus! This is the thanks I get for *rotting* in this stinking hell hole, pushing shit up hill, watching what I say, tiptoeing around, treading on eggshells, *kissing Dr. Robert Smith's arse* while you sit around laughing and squawking and barking like a freak. You didn't know if you were Arthur or Martha when you came in here and this is the thanks I get. *Now* you're upset. *Now* I've upset you. Good. *Good.* See how much *you* like it. *(He sees Robert standing in the doorway and stares.)*

ROBERT. When you use the term "Neighbour," do you mean it rhetorically or "generically"? *(Robert comes into the room, takes an orange from the bowl, sits and peels it as he talks.)* Because it's just occurred to me that when Chris talks about his "Neighbour," he might not mean literally "the people next door." Do you Chris? Nor would you mean "sibling" should you allude to a "Brother." *(Eating.)* Neighbours is Everybody isn't it? People in the street giving you a wide berth. Women on escalators holding their handbags that little bit tighter as you pass. People looking straight through you as if you're not even there. Football hooligans. Skinheads. Throwing bananas. Your workmates. Bruce and I can only *guess* at the horror of suffering from acute paranoia *and* being one of a culturally oppressed minority. What a combination. *(Pause.)* And we ask each other. Why are our mental hospitals full of young men like this? Why do you *think*? *(Pause.)*

BRUCE.   Robert-Robert-Robert-Robert-Robert-Robert-Robert ... *(Pause.)* Doctor ... *(Robert produces a prescription pad from his pocket and writes a prescription.)*

ROBERT. Why don't you report to outpatients and they'll organize you a car. *(Pause.)* Chris? Then you can go home?

CHRISTOPHER. Do you think I should?

ROBERT. Yes. You must.

CHRISTOPHER. Do you think I'm ready? Really?

ROBERT. Yes. You're ready. You can't stay in here forever. *(To Bruce.)* Can he?

BRUCE. I ... what ...

ROBERT. Do you want to get better?

CHRISTOPHER. Yeah ... I want to.

ROBERT. Then you must do what you must do. Be brave.

CHRISTOPHER. Uh?

ROBERT. Be brave.

CHRISTOPHER. "Be brave"?

ROBERT. Yes. Because you are brave. You're a very brave young man and you've done really well. This is your prescription. *(He hands Christopher the prescription.)*

CHRISTOPHER. Did you hear what he said?

BRUCE. I'm sorry. I didn't mean it.

CHRISTOPHER. Why d'you say those things, man?

BRUCE. I really am sorry.

CHRISTOPHER. My God. It really is a game of two halves with you. D'you know what I mean?

BRUCE. Are you all right?

CHRISTOPHER. What? *No.* That *hurt,* man. I can't stay in here if you're gonna say shit like that. D'you know what I mean? Running your mouth. It's *rude.*

BRUCE. I know.

CHRISTOPHER. It's *weird.*

BRUCE. Sure.

CHRISTOPHER. How would you like it?

71

BRUCE. I know … I'm sorry.

CHRISTOPHER. No you don't know. How would you like it?

ROBERT. If you'd like to make another Complaint —

CHRISTOPHER. I *am* complaining. I'm complaining to *him* and he's not even listening.

BRUCE. I … I think I need to sit down.

ROBERT. Would you like to lodge a Complaint with the Authority?

CHRISTOPHER. No. I'm OK.

ROBERT. It's really no trouble.

CHRISTOPHER. I'm all right now. *(Bruce sits. He stares. They regard him as he picks up a piece of orange peel, examines it, bites into it.)*

ROBERT. I'll get one of the nurses to book your first outpatient appointment.

CHRISTOPHER. Thanks.

ROBERT. Don't mention it.

CHRISTOPHER. No really, safe, man. I appreciate it.

ROBERT. It was the least I could do.

CHRISTOPHER. Thank you. *(Robert offers his hand and they shake hands. Bruce just stares from one to the other. Christopher goes to Bruce, suddenly staring oddly. Silence. Christopher picks up an orange.)* Have you ever stuck your dick in one of these? *(Bruce looks at him nervously.)* One time I tried it with a grapefruit. At Christmas. It's OK but it chaffs a bit. The juice stings. On the ward I seen one boy do it with bugs. Straight up. Puts a bug on the end of his willy. A cockroach. Just on the tip. He likes the way it wiggles. You think there's bugs in this?

BRUCE. I'm … sorry…?

CHRISTOPHER. Is there bugs in this?

BRUCE. Chris … please …

CHRISTOPHER. I need a girlfriend, man. D'you know what I mean? That's all I ever wanted. I just wanted somebody nice to be with. A lady. *(Silence.)*

ROBERT. Take it with you if you like.

CHRISTOPHER. Uh?

ROBERT. Take it. Be my guest. *(Pause.)* It's a gift. It's time to go home.

CHRISTOPHER. What have you done to it? What have you put

in it? What are you staring at? *(Christopher ignores the orange. He stares from Robert to Bruce suspiciously. He moves a few steps towards the door, then stops.)*

ROBERT. That's right. Off you go. Go home and listen to some reggae music. *(Christopher stares at Robert for some time. Robert eventually smiles and indicates the door. Christopher goes. Robert looks at Bruce, shakes his head, "tuts" at length.*

BRUCE. "Reggae music"?

ROBERT. What is it in Africa, "Jungle"? N'ha ha ha. *(Snorts. Bruce picks up an orange.)*

BRUCE. Well. That's that, then.

ROBERT. How do you mean "That's that"?

BRUCE. I've fucked it up, haven't I?

ROBERT. Oh I see what you mean. Well … yes.

BRUCE. I'll never make Consultant.

ROBERT. You still want to?

BRUCE. Well … of course … but …

ROBERT. Oh. *(Long silence.)*

BRUCE. Unless …

ROBERT. What's that?

BRUCE. We … don't really have to pursue this … now … do we?

ROBERT. Well I can tell you, I'm in no hurry to have the good name of my department dragged through the mud. Thank you very much.

BRUCE. No … *(Pause.)* Not to mention … not to mention your Professorship.

ROBERT. My Professorship? How does it affect that?

BRUCE. Well … it doesn't. *(Bruce carefully picks up the remains of the screwed up, torn report.)* So … where do we go from here? *(Pause.)* I mean … what's the procedure? We were getting on quite well. Until … this … disagreement.

ROBERT. It's a little more than that.

BRUCE. But it's … I mean … uh … you're a good Supervisor. And a valuable Mentor. *(Pause.)* I'm pr … I'm privileged. I'm grateful to you. *(Pause.)* For … putting me straight. *(Pause.)* One could have made a dreadful mistake. *(Pause.)* Perhaps … I could … buy you a drink … to express my gratitude. Debrief. I could read your manuscript. *(Pause.)*

ROBERT. No. I don't think we'll do that.

BRUCE. W ... why not?

ROBERT. Well. The thing is ... I'll tell you something. I don't like you, Bruce. You talk too much. You get in the way. *(Silence.)* You see, sick people come to me. All creeds and colors. They are suffering. They go away again and they no longer suffer. Because of me. All because of me. And there's nothing wrong with that. Is there?

BRUCE. Who do you think you are? God?

ROBERT. How does Archbishop of Canterbury sound? N'ha ha ha. You will not be employed by this Authority again. We made a mistake. It's a little Darwinian, I admit, nevertheless. Goodbye. *(He hands Bruce the orange.)* You can eat it on the train. *(Bruce stares at the orange in his hand. He slumps in his chair. He peels the orange. He stares at Robert. Robert goes.)*

BRUCE. I want to make a Complaint. *(Robert stops.)* I'd like to lodge a Complaint with the Authority.

ROBERT. Sorry?

BRUCE. I'm ready to give you a Statement. What's the procedure for that? *(Bruce bites into the orange. They stare at each other. Blackout.)*

End of Play

PROPERTY LIST

Water cooler and cups (CHRISTOPHER)
Cup of coffee (ROBERT)
Packet of cigarettes and lighter (ROBERT)
Glass bowl with several oranges (BRUCE)
Cigarettes (CHRISTOPHER)
Wallet and folded newspaper clipping (CHRISTOPHER)
Report (BRUCE)
Mobile phone (ROBERT)
Diary (ROBERT)
Hold-all (CHRISTOPHER)
File and pamphlet (BRUCE)
Prescription pad and pen (ROBERT)

NEW PLAYS

★ **MONTHS ON END by Craig Pospisil.** In comic scenes, one for each month of the year, we follow the intertwined worlds of a circle of friends and family whose lives are poised between happiness and heartbreak. "...a triumph...these twelve vignettes all form crucial pieces in the eternal puzzle known as human relationships, an area in which the playwright displays an assured knowledge that spans deep sorrow to unbounded happiness." *–Ann Arbor News.* "...rings with emotional truth, humor...[an] endearing contemplation on love...entertaining and satisfying." *–Oakland Press.* [5M, 5W] ISBN: 0-8222-1892-5

★ **GOOD THING by Jessica Goldberg.** Brings us into the households of John and Nancy Roy, forty-something high-school guidance counselors whose marriage has been increasingly on the rocks and Dean and Mary, recent graduates struggling to make their way in life. "...a blend of gritty social drama, poetic humor and unsubtle existential contemplation..." *–Variety.* [3M, 3W] ISBN: 0-8222-1869-0

★ **THE DEAD EYE BOY by Angus MacLachlan.** Having fallen in love at their Narcotics Anonymous meeting, Billy and Shirley-Diane are striving to overcome the past together. But their relationship is complicated by the presence of Sorin, Shirley-Diane's fourteen-year-old son, a damaged reminder of her dark past. "...a grim, insightful portrait of an unmoored family..." *–NY Times.* "MacLachlan's play isn't for the squeamish, but then, tragic stories delivered at such an unrelenting fever pitch rarely are." *–Variety.* [1M, 1W, 1 boy] ISBN: 0-8222-1844-5

★ **[SIC] by Melissa James Gibson.** In adjacent apartments three young, ambitious neighbors come together to discuss, flirt, argue, share their dreams and plan their futures with unequal degrees of deep hopefulness and abject despair. "A work...concerned with the sound and power of language..." *–NY Times.* "...a wonderfully original take on urban friendship and the comedy of manners—a *Design for Living* for our times..." *–NY Observer.* [3M, 2W] ISBN: 0-8222-1872-0

★ **LOOKING FOR NORMAL by Jane Anderson.** Roy and Irma's twenty-five-year marriage is thrown into turmoil when Roy confesses that he is actually a woman trapped in a man's body, forcing the couple to wrestle with the meaning of their marriage and the delicate dynamics of family. "Jane Anderson's bittersweet transgender domestic comedy-drama ...is thoughtful and touching and full of wit and wisdom. A real audience pleaser." *–Hollywood Reporter.* [5M, 4W] ISBN: 0-8222-1857-7

★ **ENDPAPERS by Thomas McCormack.** The regal Joshua Maynard, the old and ailing head of a mid-sized, family-owned book-publishing house in New York City, must name a successor. One faction in the house backs a smart, "pragmatic" manager, the other faction a smart, "sensitive" editor and both factions fear what the other's man could do to this house— and to them. "If Kaufman and Hart had undertaken a comedy about the publishing business, they might have written *Endpapers*...a breathlessly fast, funny, and thoughtful comedy ...keeps you amused, guessing, and often surprised...profound in its empathy for the paradoxes of human nature." *–NY Magazine.* [7M, 4W] ISBN: 0-8222-1908-5

★ **THE PAVILION by Craig Wright.** By turns poetic and comic, romantic and philosophical, this play asks old lovers to face the consequences of difficult choices made long ago. "The script's greatest strength lies in the genuineness of its feeling." *–Houston Chronicle.* "Wright's perceptive, gently witty writing makes this familiar situation fresh and thoroughly involving." *–Philadelphia Inquirer.* [2M, 1W (flexible casting)] ISBN: 0-8222-1898-4

DRAMATISTS PLAY SERVICE, INC.
440 Park Avenue South, New York, NY 10016 212-683-8960 Fax 212-213-1539
postmaster@dramatists.com www.dramatists.com

NEW PLAYS

★ **BE AGGRESSIVE by Annie Weisman.** Vista Del Sol is paradise, sandy beaches, avocado-lined streets. But for seventeen-year-old cheerleader Laura, everything changes when her mother is killed in a car crash, and she embarks on a journey to the Spirit Institute of the South where she can learn "cheer" with Bible belt intensity. "…filled with lingual gymnastics…stylized rapid-fire dialogue…" –*Variety*. "…a new, exciting, and unique voice in the American theatre…" –*BackStage West*. [1M, 4W, extras] ISBN: 0-8222-1894-1

★ **FOUR by Christopher Shinn.** Four people struggle desperately to connect in this quiet, sophisticated, moving drama. "…smart, broken-hearted…Mr. Shinn has a precocious and forgiving sense of how power shifts in the game of sexual pursuit…He promises to be a playwright to reckon with…" –*NY Times*. "A voice emerges from an American place. It's got humor, sadness and a fresh and touching rhythm that tell of the loneliness and secrets of life…[a] poetic, haunting play." –*NY Post*. [3M, 1W] ISBN: 0-8222-1850-X

★ **WONDER OF THE WORLD by David Lindsay-Abaire.** A madcap picaresque involving Niagara Falls, a lonely tour-boat captain, a pair of bickering private detectives and a husband's dirty little secret. "Exceedingly whimsical and playfully wicked. Winning and genial. A top-drawer production." –*NY Times*. "Full frontal lunacy is on display. A most assuredly fresh and hilarious tragicomedy of marital discord run amok…absolutely hysterical…" –*Variety*. [3M, 4W (doubling)] ISBN: 0-8222-1863-1

★ **QED by Peter Parnell.** Nobel Prize-winning physicist and all-around genius Richard Feynman holds forth with captivating wit and wisdom in this fascinating biographical play that originally starred Alan Alda. "QED is a seductive mix of science, human affections, moral courage, and comic eccentricity. It reflects on, among other things, death, the absence of God, travel to an unexplored country, the pleasures of drumming, and the need to know and understand." –*NY Magazine*. "Its rhythms correspond to the way that people—even geniuses—approach and avoid highly emotional issues, and it portrays Feynman with affection and awe." –*The New Yorker*. [1M, 1W] ISBN: 0-8222-1924-7

★ **UNWRAP YOUR CANDY by Doug Wright.** Alternately chilling and hilarious, this deliciously macabre collection of four bedtime tales for adults is guaranteed to keep you awake for nights on end. "Engaging and intellectually satisfying…a treat to watch." –*NY Times*. "Fiendishly clever. Mordantly funny and chilling. Doug Wright teases, freezes and zaps us." –*Village Voice*. "Four bite-size plays that bite back." –*Variety*. [flexible casting] ISBN: 0-8222-1871-2

★ **FURTHER THAN THE FURTHEST THING by Zinnie Harris.** On a remote island in the middle of the Atlantic secrets are buried. When the outside world comes calling, the islanders find their world blown apart from the inside as well as beyond. "Harris winningly produces an intimate and poetic, as well as political, family saga." –*Independent (London)*. "Harris' enthralling adventure of a play marks a departure from stale, well-furrowed theatrical terrain." –*Evening Standard (London)*. [3M, 2W] ISBN: 0-8222-1874-7

★ **THE DESIGNATED MOURNER by Wallace Shawn.** The story of three people living in a country where what sort of books people like to read and how they choose to amuse themselves becomes both firmly personal and unexpectedly entangled with questions of survival. "This is a playwright who does not just tell you what it is like to be arrested at night by goons or to fall morally apart and become an aimless yet weirdly contented ghost yourself. He has the originality to make you feel it." –*Times (London)*. "A fascinating play with beautiful passages of writing…" –*Variety*. [2M, 1W] ISBN: 0-8222-1848-8

DRAMATISTS PLAY SERVICE, INC.
440 Park Avenue South, New York, NY 10016 212-683-8960 Fax 212-213-1539
postmaster@dramatists.com www.dramatists.com

NEW PLAYS

★ **SHEL'S SHORTS by Shel Silverstein.** Lauded poet, songwriter and author of children's books, the incomparable Shel Silverstein's short plays are deeply infused with the same wicked sense of humor that made him famous. "…[a] childlike honesty and twisted sense of humor."   · of dread
give [*She*   —*Boston*
Phoenix.

★ **AN A**   ome to
the dark   where
the mos   inative
plays va   shows
off Silve   a clear
apprecia   asting]
ISBN: 0

★ **WHE**   section
of the   p wit.
"…Shan   rtainly
potent..   " —*NY*
Times. [

★ **A FI**   omedy-
drama tl   ed by a
cast of f   era star
Adelina   o awe-
some he   ght call
an every   [10M,
3W] ISI

★ **BRE**   Prix, a
Bronx n   matu-
rity at th   ic visit,
where n   r, terse
vernacul

★ **THE**   d Earl,
are bre   Mexico
home   s out
of the   nents
…She

★ **TH**   span-
ning f   ining
mono   ulous
way..

★ **TH**   aking
homaş   n't let
them   l rev-
elatioı   gering
beaut   7